CRUISE MATE

...AND THE VOYAGE CONTINUES

THE BOOK ABOUT HOW, WHY, WHEN AND WHERE TO CRUISE

Larree Chetelat

Second Edition, Completely Revised

Pony Publishing, Parker, Colorado

CRUISE MATE...AND THE VOYAGE CONTINUES

Cruise Mate...And The Voyage Continues takes you through the steps of a cruise; how to plan, prepare, select a cruise ship and what to expect on board.

By Larree Chetelat

Published by:

Pony Publishing
10532 Stoneflower Drive, Ste 33
Parker, Colorado 80134 U.S.A.

Cruise Mate...And The Voyage Continues,
a guide for cruising.

Copyright ©1999 by Larree Chetelat.

First Printing 1997

Second Printing 1999 - 2000 Completely Revised

Printed and bound in the United States of America. All rights reserved. No part of this book may be reproduced in any form or by any electronic and/or mechanical means including information storage and retrieval systems without permission in writing from the author, except by a reviewer, who may quote brief passages in a review.

Library of Congress Catalogue Card
Number: 99-94783

ISBN 0-9658398-2-6

CRUISE MATE...AND THE VOYAGE CONTINUES

This book is dedicated to the memory of my mother, Mabel S. Chetelat, who loved to travel and who stirred my interests in the exciting world of travel.

and to...

all who cruise or would like to cruise... may your voyage continue.

TABLE OF CONTENTS

CHAPTER ONE

THE CRUISE WORLD.............................. 1
   An Introduction................................ 1
   Safety and Environmental Programs......... 8
   Navigation.. 10

CHAPTER TWO

PLANNING AND PREPARING.................. 12
   Planning for Your Cruise..................... 12
   Cruise Line Brochures......................... 13
   The Internet...................................... 16
   Cabin Selection.................................. 16
   Best Time to Book.............................. 20
   Cruise Experience.............................. 20
   Tips for Honeymooners....................... 22
   Start Preparing.................................. 23
   Your Own Cruise Mate Card................. 24
   Motion Sickness................................ 25
   Medical Preparations.......................... 26
   Communications................................ 27
   Travel Documents.............................. 28
   Car Use.. 29
   Travel Sense..................................... 30
      Sense of Purpose........................... 31
      Sense of Direction.......................... 31
      Sense of Humor............................. 31
      Common Sense............................. 33

CHAPTER THREE

TRAVEL AGENT ASSOCIATION............... 34
   Selecting a Travel Agent..................... 34
   The booking...................................... 39
   Deposit.. 43

TABLE OF CONTENTS (Continued)

Cancellations...... 45
Travel Packet...... 45
Insurance...... 47
Late Contract for a Cruise...... 49

CHAPTER FOUR

TYPES OF CRUISES, WHERE AND WHEN... 50
Types of Cruises...... 50
Repositioning Cruise...... 52
Where and When to Cruise...... 53
Selecting an Itinerary...... 56
  Alaska...... 56
  Caribbean...... 58
    Eastern Caribbean...... 59
    Western Caribbean...... 60
    Southern Caribbean...... 61
  Bermuda...... 63
  New England and Canada...... 64
  Panama Canal...... 65
  Overseas...... 67

CHAPTER FIVE

SELECTING A CRUISE LINE AND SHIP...... 69
Cruise Ship Pricing...... 69
Cruise Ship Size...... 71
Where Ships Are Built...... 72
Overview of Mid-Price Ships...... 73
A "Thumbnail Sketch"...... 73
What's Right For You...... 75
Ship Selection...... 77
Grading Ships...... 80
Passenger Age Scale...... 81
Ship Roominess &Passenger Space Ratio... 82

Holland America Line...... 84
  The World of Holland America...... 86
    Passengers...... 86
    Ships...... 87

TABLE OF CONTENTS (Continued)

Royal Caribbean International.................. 88
   The World of Royal Caribbean.............. 89
      Passengers...................................... 90
      Ships... 90

Celebrity Cruises..................................... 92
   The World of Celebrity....................... 93
      Passengers...................................... 93
      Ships... 94

Princess Cruises..................................... 95
   The World of Princess........................ 96
      Passengers...................................... 96
      Ships... 97

Disney Cruise Line................................. 98
   The World of Disney......................... 99
      Passengers...................................... 99
      Ships... 100

Norwegian Cruise Line........................... 100
   The World of Norwegian................... 101
      Passengers...................................... 101
      Ships... 101

Costa Cruises... 102
   The World of Costa........................... 103
      Passengers...................................... 104
      Ships... 104

Carnival Cruise Lines............................. 105
   The World of Carnival....................... 106
      Passengers...................................... 106
      Ships... 107

Orient Lines.. 109
   The World of Orient.......................... 110
      Passengers...................................... 110
      Ship.. 111

TABLE OF CONTENTS (Continued)

American Hawaii Cruises...... 111
   The World of American Hawaii...... 112
      Passengers...... 112
      Ship...... 113

Overview of Luxury Ships...... 113
Luxury Cruise Lines...... 114

Ship Photos...... 115-118

Crystal Cruises...... 119
   The World of Crystal...... 120
      Passengers...... 120
      Ships...... 121

Cunard Line, Ltd...... 121
   The World of Cunard...... 122
      Passengers...... 122
      Ships...... 123

Radisson Seven Seas Cruises...... 124
   The World of Radisson...... 124
      Passengers...... 124
      Ships...... 125

Seabourn Cruise Line...... 126
   The World of Seabourn...... 126
      Passengers...... 127
      Ships...... 127

Silversea Cruises...... 128
   The World of Silversea...... 128
      Passengers...... 129
      Ships...... 129

Windstar Cruises, "The Tall Ships"...... 130
   The World of Windstar...... 131
      Passengers...... 131
      Tall Ships...... 131

TABLE OF CONTENTS (Continued)

Delta Queen Steamboat Co. River Cruises.... 132
    The World of The Delta Queen Company.. 133
        Passengers....................................... 135
        Boats... 135

River Cruises.. 136
Barge "Cruising".. 136
Freighter and Cargo Ships..................... 137

CHAPTER SIX

TRANSPORTATION AND HOTELS.............. 140
    Cruise Line Air/Sea Total Packages........... 140
    Scheduling Transportation and Hotels........ 142
    Hotel Safety Tips.................................. 146

CHAPTER SEVEN

PACKING TIPS... 148
    Packing... 148
    Dress For Ladies................................. 152
    Dress For Gentlemen........................... 155
    Packing for Dinner Dress...................... 156
    Suggested Packing Checklist.................. 157
    Seven Day List for Ladies,
        Gentlemen and Family...................... 157
    Seven Day List for Gentlemen................ 158
    Seven Day Suggested List for
        Ladies... 159
    Things To Do At Home Before
        You Leave.................................... 160

CHAPTER EIGHT

EMBARKATION AND LEARNING
    THE SHIP.. 162
    Planning Your Arrival.......................... 162
    Boarding Procedures........................... 163
    Valuables... 166
    Learning Your Way Around the Ship......... 167

TABLE OF CONTENTS (Continued)

Devising a Locator Card................ 169
"Knots" and a "Log".................... 172

CHAPTER NINE

SHIPBOARD DRESS AND DINING.............. 174
    Dress, Customs and Etiquette................ 174
    Dining....................................... 178
    Dining Room Etiquette........................ 181
    Gratuities(Only a Guideline)................. 184

CHAPTER TEN

SHIPBOARD ACTIVITIES........................ 188
    Entertainment................................ 188
    Keeping in Shape............................. 190
    Games and Casino............................. 191
    Safety and Rules............................. 192
    Lifeboat Drill............................... 193
    General Ship Operating Procedures............ 195
    Ship's Crew.................................. 196
    On board Shopping............................ 199

CHAPTER ELEVEN

EXCURSIONS AND PORT ACTIVITIES.............. 201
    The Cruise Package........................... 201
    Booking the Tours............................ 204
    Tendering.................................... 205
    Port Shopping................................ 206
    Time Changes................................. 207

CHAPTER TWELVE

DISEMBARKATION.............................. 208
    The Cruise Conclusion........................ 208
    Preparing to Disembark....................... 210
    Wrap-up...................................... 214

TABLE OF CONTENTS (Continued)

APPENDIX.. 216

    Nautical Glossary............................. 217
    Index.. 231
    Cruise Mates and Notes...................... 234
    Reorders... 235

ABOUT THE AUTHOR

Larree Chetelat was graduated from Colorado State University and served as a pilot in the United States Air Force and then as a Systems Engineer in the Aerospace Industry. During his service with the Air Force, he served in several combat theaters and traveled throughout the world.

Larree is not a travel agent. The information contained here is based on his own experience (therefore unofficial) and the association with cruise passengers, cruise line officers, staff and crew members and the procedures with sailing on the various major cruise lines. He became interested in the cruise world during his years as an engineer with aerospace reading books and brochures on cruising. The first time he sailed, he was hooked.

Larree's first book, *Cruise Mate,* published in 1997, was well received and was suggested reading by several different travel agencies to their cruise clients. Larree has given numerous cruise lectures on board several major cruise lines. Many questions and comments received at his lectures and on his first book have gone into this second book, which has been expanded. Larree has also written numerous technical books, magazine and newspaper articles.

PREFACE

I am excited about cruising! I have been on many cruises in the past few years sailing on several different cruise lines. My wife and I have cruised the Caribbean, Panama Canal, Canada, New England, Mexico, Alaska, Hawaii, Bermuda, the Pacific, Atlantic and Europe as well as visits to the Far East.

Our staterooms have been located in the ship's bow, stern, middle, very low, high with a veranda/balcony, in a deluxe cabin and suites with butler service, We have sailed on ship's "Maiden Voyages" and during several "Inaugural Voyage" years. We have also sailed on older ships. We have sailed back to back on two and three different ships. We have dined with the main seating and the late seating. We were selected as guests at the Captain's table on several cruise lines. On one cruise, we had dinner with the Captain during the entire cruise. This is considered a privilege, an honor and is a wonderful experience.

These cruises have provided a life of excitement, travel, excellent food, superb entertainment, security of the ship hotel and a lifestyle of activities for both day and night. The friendships and camaraderie are treasures that will remain for years to come. I have discovered that a ship itself is not necessarily a destination, but a journey, process and excitement of the voyage to be richly enjoyed.

PREFACE (Continued)

I have written this book based on my experience with travel and cruising. My wife and I have traveled extensively meeting people who have had some misconceptions and questions about the cruise world. It is evident to us from conversations with travel agents and many other people that the information we have gained would greatly assist first time cruisers, cruisers who do not cruise often and even some of the veteran "old salts."

I feel I can share my experiences so they will help make your cruising more enjoyable. So enjoy the book...

Happy cruising!

Larree Chetelat

ACKNOWLEDGEMENT

Nearly all the material in this book is based on my own experiences and reflect my personal opinions about the cruise world. There have been many cruise passengers, travel agents, cruise line offices, on board ship officers, staff and crew members who were interviewed to gather information for this book. Many of these people are considered authorities in the business. It would be impossible to mention them all, but my thanks to them. Also, an extensive amount of cruise line brochures and press/media kits were consulted for ship specifications, cruise line information and procedures.

Copy editing by Dona Chetelat
Text content review by Edith Taylor, CTC, ACC
Cover by Nick Zelinger

DISCLAIMER

Cruise Mate...And The Voyage Continues is an unofficial cruise book written to provide helpful information only. The author does not intend to render legal or professional advice or usurp cruise line brochures in rendering important information concerning the methods in planning, booking, performing and terminating a cruise. We suggest you consult with your travel agent for all your travel needs.

The author has attempted to write this book as accurate and comprehensive as possible. Due to the extremely viable and constant changing cruise world, dates and conditions will change rapidly. Therefore the book should be used as a reference for the cruise enthusiast to better plan and understand the cruise world and ultimately have a more enjoyable cruise.

The purpose of *Cruise Mate...And The Voyage Continues* is to assist a person or persons in the "how, why, when and where" of cruising. We do not accept liability or responsibility from any person for loss or damage caused, or alleged to be caused, directly or indirectly by the *Cruise Mate...And The Voyage Continues* content. If you do not wish to accept these conditions, please disregard the contents and return the book.

CHAPTER ONE

THE CRUISE WORLD

AN INTRODUCTION

A cruise vacation is a wonderful experience...and you can be a very special part of it!

Today's cruise ships sail the world over! Cruising is the "once-upon-a-time story" that keeps getting better and better! During the last ten or twelve years, the cruise industry has grown by leaps and bounds. This creates a need for a handbook to help cruise enthusiasts plan, prepare and enjoy a great cruise on the magnificent ships of the world. Now is the time to take that cruise you have been thinking about, or that follow-on cruise and get a glimpse of the "good life." *Cruise Mate* will help you do just that. It will help you select the cruise just right for you. This is very important because any ship at any price level could be the special one for you. You cannot place a price on happiness, but it costs less when cruising!

Each and every cruise ship creates an atmosphere that is strictly "that" particular ship. This can be called a ship's own personality, style, ambiance, environment, experience, or that certain air of its facilities and crew -- or call it whatever you like. Ships can have a formal, semiformal, casual, contemporary, classic, elegant, austere, old salt, champagne and caviar, beer and pretzels, cluttered or open space atmosphere. Some ships may contain famous art, statues, antiques, fine furniture and beautiful fresh flower arrangements. Others may dazzle the guests with abstract or glitzy way-out lights and displays. You need to select a cruise line and ship that best fits your lifestyle; a ship that has an atmosphere just right for you.

Cruising on a beautiful ship is exciting! The cruise industry has become more and more popular in recent years. The pace of modernization has been rapid. New classy ships are being built each year with more and more people sailing the seas. The competition between cruise lines has also been raised to a higher level. The cruise lines are after your business. They want to offer you choices and want you to return for another cruise.

Taking to the high seas in record numbers, travelers representing a broad spectrum of the American and Canadian public are putting to bed the myth that cruising is an exclusive experience reserved for the wealthy and elderly. Nearly eight million sea-goers are sailing each year. You can be part of this great way to travel. The oceans are a great source of excitement, adventure and romance. No frustration about finding a place to dine, five star cuisine is prepared and served in a beautiful manner. No question where you will stop for a hotel or what entertainment to seek. No concern of how much to pay at a nightclub, Broadway show or theater, or even a movie. It is all prepaid and you know the costs up-front...*And just think, you unpack and pack just one time, yet you visit many wonderful and exciting places!* No wonder over 85 percent of people who go on a cruise, will repeat and repeat.

Contrary to common misconceptions, cruises cater to a diverse demographic mix, not just wealthy senior citizens. The average age of cruise passengers has dropped considerably over the past twenty years. Most ships have a multi national crew who make the cruise much more interesting

There are several types of cruise lines and many types of cruise ships. The *Cruise Mate* will help you decide on a particular cruise based on your lifestyle, desires or needs. Several cruise lines will be discussed, giving you tips on how to select a particular cruise line and a specific ship. There is information on the best time of year for a cruise and how to select an itinerary.

A very important area that is not covered adequately in other books is "tell it like it is" travel agent, passenger, cruise line, cruise ship and crew responsibilities to one another. This includes safety, shipboard rules, dress, customs and etiquette. Even tips on dining and how to use the ten or twelve pieces of silverware at your dinner table.

There are so many activities available on cruise ships, sometimes we lose track of why we are on the cruise. We must have a sense of purpose for our cruise. *Cruise Mate* will discuss how to relax and plan excursions and tours for a fun vacation. There is no reason to leave your cruise vacation stressed.

Cruise Mate does not rate the cruise lines, however, we do give you information so you can make a good, educated decision. We have been able to compare several major cruise lines and many ships first hand. We have met and talked with many other cruise passengers, taking notes to learn more about their impressions of various other ships and cruise lines. We made evaluation notes of the ships we have sailed on and recorded inputs from ship's officers, staff and crew members. *Cruise Mate* also has added comments and recommendations to this research from a variety of different travel agents. Along with this, we have secured media/press kits and brochures from many of the cruise lines and have extracted pertinent information. We have also included some information concerning The Delta Queen Steamboat Company river cruises on the inland waterways, plus some general information on barge and freighter travel..

It is very difficult to be bored! The cruising industry is alive, well and a great experience! When properly informed there is a vast amount of prospective customers for the cruise lines and this is the year to begin. Regardless of whether you are a child or over 70, you will love it! Most cruise lines have provisions and procedures to assist the physically challenged. Discuss this with your travel agent.

A cruise is a cornucopia of activities to be involved with, a time to relax or enjoy a good book at pool or ocean side. You will see, smell, hear and feel the romance and mystery of the sea. Cruising is a time to get to know each other all over again, rekindle romance, enjoy friends and enhance further bonding of parents, children and spouses for the good quality of life. A special camaraderie can easily be developed with certain fellow passengers.

Your cruise experience will be directly related to the ship's management, activities and how you, the cruise-goer, becomes involved. This includes the very important first impression of the ship, stateroom, crew and service personnel. Also, the entertainment, the decor and how passenger's problems are handled by ship personnel. But, remember it is nearly impossible to please everyone all the time, however, ship's staff makes the attempt. You will mentally judge the cuisine and the service or method the food is served. Passengers can be treated to a lobster tail, flamed dessert, baked Alaska or can partake of a lavish buffet, or enjoy a hot dog, hamburger, taco or pizza at pool side. Some ships have free ice cream, and even popcorn to take to the free movies. Ships respond to today's trend toward dishes lighter in cholesterol, fat and sodium by offering food choices. For the more health conscious, cruise lines are providing a potpourri of guilt-free options to include vegetarian menu choices, fresh fruits and natural snacks.

On a land vacation it is not easy to find a great restaurant each and every time you dine out. At sea, every meal, every time is a treat to the culinary arts. It does not matter whether you prefer elegant five course meals, casual dining, lean fare or vegetarian, today's cruise liners make it a point to provide their guests with an array of foods to tempt every palate. With more and more cruisers enjoying relaxed, less formal cruise vacations, many cruise ships are combining formal nights with informal and casual. They also offer separate dining options with full course menus for the casual dinner guest.

Cruise lines offer a variety of great fun, relaxation and enjoyable experiences that are hard to duplicate anywhere. A majority of the ships have movies, great entertainment, dance instruction, learning and enrichment lecture sessions, classics, library and beauty salons with body massages. Most have great swimming pools and a complete fitness center. Excursions at ports are available at additional cost. All this and much more is available. The ships have port lecturers who advise you of many good purchases at a soon to be visited port, places for lunch and situations to avoid. There are activities for children, singles, couples and all age groups. You can pursue your hobbies, reading, bridge, puzzles, physical fitness, sit and just relax plus many other interests during a cruise. The Cruise Director has something for everyone!

The ship's safety is great for singles. A lady can go by herself to a disco, bar, cocktail lounge, dance floor, show production, movie or elsewhere and then retire to the safety of her cabin. No driving required. Some ships employ gentlemen hosts who will dance with and escort single ladies at ship functions and dance classes. Male and female singles can make friends at the dinner table, dance classes, trivia games and casino. Singles should not over-look associating with married couples as they can be good match makers. They can introduce singles to other singles. Have a friendly smile and do not be afraid to join in. You can also request to be seated at a dinner table with other singles. The atmosphere on board ship is friendly and more sociable than a hotel on land.

There is a large spectrum of cruise lines and cruise ships. When selecting a cruise line, cruise ship, itinerary, and dates for sailing, there are a number of considerations. Of course this depends on your timing and cost of the cruise. And don't worry about sea sickness. Nearly all ships have stabilizers to help hold the ship from roll. Less than 3% of the passengers feel the effect of motion sickness, and then only for a short duration. Your chances are probably greater of becoming sun burned than sea sick.

SAFETY AND ENVIRONMENTAL PROGRAMS

Cruise lines are totally committed to the safety and security of its passengers. The law in 1894 for life boats was based on ship size and not number of passengers, thus the serious consequences of the Titanic. The cruise lines now support and adhere to stringent, internationally agreed upon standards for the design, construction and operation of all ocean vessels as set forth by the International Maritime Organization (IMO). The IMO is a specialized agency of the United Nations in the Safety of Life at Sea (SOLAS) convention. SOLAS was first drafted during January 1914 and is revised continually. It was updated in 1948, 1960, 1974 and October 1997. SOLAS, among other requirements, directs compliance with lifesaving equipment, stringent fire safety/fire fighting, crew competency, ship control, stability, watertight integrity, structural, safety management, navigation, and certain environmental protection. In North America, the cruise industry also cooperates fully with the U.S. Coast Guard, which is empowered by Congress to inspect all foreign-flag vessels operating from North American ports and to issue a Control Verification Certificate, without which a foreign-flag ship would be prohibited from embarking U.S. passengers.

Cruise lines register with foreign flag countries to avoid high American corporate taxes and other U.S. restrictions. Generally, foreign flag countries have jurisdiction over their flag ships in international waters. The United States asserts jurisdiction in its territorial waters.

Each cruise line self inspects to keep safety and security utmost in their operation. While on a cruise, you may witness a safety exercise at one of the ports of call when most passengers are off the ship. The captain may simulate an on board fire or other malfunction and the crew must respond quickly and accurately. This will be graded and critiqued.

As of 1990, all ships on any waters must meet what are known as the MARPOL standards, which are promulgated by the International Convention for the Prevention of Pollution from Ships. An international law, the MARPOL Treaty governs waste disposal in a marine environment. All cruise ships are inspected and monitored by the flag state and the U. S. Coast Guard for compliance. The standards divide water into four marine zones, depending upon the proximity to shore. Discharge is severely restricted and most refuge is stored within the ship until docking on land. Reducing waste, storage, recycling, environmental precautions and conservation are closely managed actions by all cruise lines. Stiff fines are imposed if cruise lines are found guilty of violations.

NAVIGATION

Today's ships have the most up-to-date and sophisticated state-of-the-art navigational systems. The accurate Global Positioning System (GPS) ties in with other electronic navigation aids that make ship navigation a very precise art. If you have a chance to visit the bridge of a ship during a cruise, do it. You will be amazed how automated and simple the operation is for command and control of the ship. The ship's heading and course are predetermined and all automatic. The exact position of the ship is always known and continually updated. Other ocean traffic is carefully monitored. Distance to ports is also kept current so the time of arrival can be controlled with ship speed. The bridge officers periodically receive current weather reports and are genuinely concerned with passenger and ship safety. Of course, also important is the guest's responsibility to the ship, captain, staff and crew. Rules and procedures must be followed by all passengers for their safety and the overall safety, consideration and respect of other passengers.

Enjoy *Cruise Mate.* It is easy reading and the information will be very helpful to you. It follows the order of planning, preparing, enjoying and concluding a cruise. A Nautical Glossary is included in the back of the book. Do not over-look visiting the glossary, it has some very interesting facts.

(Note: When referring to this book's title, "*Cruise Mate...And The Voyage Continues*," the author will shorten the title and use only the name "*Cruise Mate.* ")

CHAPTER TWO

PLANNING AND PREPARING

PLANNING FOR YOUR CRUISE

The preceding chapter was an introduction to the cruise industry listing a few areas your *Cruise Mate* will be covering throughout the book. The fun, security and lifestyle are there for you to enjoy so be sure to plan and prepare properly for your cruise.

This chapter provides useful information for the cruise traveler who is attempting to sift through the multitude of brochures and advertising to select and enjoy an exciting and satisfying cruise.

The planning and preparing for a cruise are two of the most important activities you can do to make your cruise enjoyable.

CRUISE LINE BROCHURES

Cruise lines prepare handsome brochures with great write-ups to advertise their ships. They describe various cruises by displaying colorful art and photos of ships and travel destinations. The ship names, layouts and sailing dates are located according to destinations/ports. There is a column of stateroom categories with a listed price. These prices can be used as a comparison with other cruise lines. Stated prices should not be the price you pay for your cruise. A good travel agent can contract a better price and sometimes an upgrade from a lower priced stateroom. Refer to Chapter Three, Travel Agent Responsibilities.

Brochures are available at the travel agent's office. Choose the ones of interest, take them home and leisurely look over them. It is fun to thumb through the pages of exciting photos and details displaying ships and destinations. Sometimes brochures may not cover your individual questions so jot down any questions you may have to ask the travel agent.

The cover of the brochure is labeled according to destinations. They may be entitled for destinations such as Europe, Caribbean, Alaska, Panama Canal, Far East, South America, British Isles, Scandinavia and more. Have a general idea where you want to go and a time frame before

PLANNING AND PREPARING

you return to the travel agent for additional discussions and guidance. Brochures will help with these decisions. If possible be a little flexible, some cruise lines offer special rates for certain times, ships and itineraries.

After scanning the brochure and you are ready to get serious, start at the table of contents and review information by ships, dates/times and itineraries. The middle part of the brochure will show you either colorful photos or art conceptions of what is available for that particular cruise area noted on the front of the brochure. For a certain itinerary such as the Western Caribbean, a graphic picture is shown of the islands the ship will visit. Category, prices and sailing dates will be listed according to year and season. Prices for a third or fourth person in one cabin will also be shown in small print. On the small chart containing the ports and time schedules, note the dates the ship sails. This all varies from ship to ship.

Towards the end of the brochure are ship's deck plans. Contained here will be either full page or fold-out diagrams of the various named decks, some statistics and a column of categories with prices. Certain cabin diagrams are depicted sometimes with square feet shown. There is information on ship dimensions, weight, capacity and a detailed layout of the ship facilities by deck and category. These layouts show where areas are located on the ship and what cabins are available relative to other facilities on board. In the bottom or top corner of the page will be keys to the little figures in each cabin. One may indicate a cabin has a third or fourth pullman berth. It may show connecting cabins or physically challenged cabins. It is important to pay special attention to the diagrams of each deck. Always ask questions to know exactly where your cabin is located. Some decks have partially obstructed or totally obstructed views either from lifeboats (tenders) or other ship equipment. Will your cabin be an inside or outside view? Changing locations once you are on board, is seldom possible.

Examine the ship's diagram in the brochure very carefully. For example: forward on lower decks, near the bow some cabins may have portholes instead of a large window. This should be displayed on the diagram. However, the cost may be less and portholes acceptable. If you prefer not to have portholes, you would not want to select these cabins.

Near the back of the brochure is information on terms and conditions of the cruise. There is information concerning the air/sea package, hotel and other cruise requirements. Also, there are cruise line costs listed for flying from various cities. Other subjects addressed are contract conditions, customs, times for dinner, dress suggestions and requirements, how to be reached while aboard ship, embarkation and sailing times. Sometimes, there is a quick reference pictorial on the inside back cover showing all the cruise line ships, year sailing dates and itineraries in graph

PLANNING AND PREPARING

form. Each cruise line has a specific way of organizing their brochure. Cruise lines also offer a travel video that can be purchased for approximately $10.00. It will give you a preview of the activities, staterooms, dining and entertainment. Normally an 800 number is provided in cruise brochures to order the video.

THE INTERNET

The Internet can be searched and consulted for general cruise information. There are many sources to review on the Internet. Sometimes this can be of some help and other times all available data can be confusing. If you are an Internet fan, our suggestion is do some Internet research. However, we recommend you work and book with a "live" travel agent. The travel agent can advise, assist and accomplish special requests, as well as protect you. Some complaints have come from people who book through the Internet. The problems involved air, sea and land reservations and connections. It is very important to keep all receipts.

CABIN SELECTION

Varying somewhat with each ship are normally five to eighteen stacked levels or decks. Ship levels are called decks and not floors. Some decks contain many of the cabins (also called staterooms). One important thing to remember, you will not spend a lot of time in your cabin, especially on three, four or seven day cruises. There are too many activities available on the outside. On a ten, twelve, fourteen, sixteen day or longer cruise, you will spend more time in your cabin. If there are more days at sea as opposed to port days, you will also tend to relax in your cabin more often. There are several aspects to be considered when selecting a cabin. Remember, there are many areas inside and outside the ship where you can quietly relax and enjoy, such as various lounges, library or the Promenade Deck.

Near the middle level of the ship is the Promenade Deck. On many ships this deck has a walkway around the ship. The cruise enthusiast can walk to exercise, sightsee, relax in the deck chairs with a good book or even snooze. If cabins are on the Promenade Deck they will have tinted or reflective windows but will not view the open sea directly because of the width of the Promenade Deck. During the evening you can draw your drapes for privacy. Rooms such as these are normally priced slightly less, and for the most part are fine for cruising.

Brochures will describe locations and layout of the ship's cabins as well as pertinent information concerning the ship. This assists in determining a cabin location based on category and price. Category, cruise length and season will normally determine the cost of your cruise. The inside cabins located at the lowest levels far forward and aft are the least expensive. The outside cabins (ocean view) in these locations are slightly higher in price. You can experience slightly more movement of the ship at extreme forward or aft locations than at mid ship.

When cruising in an inside cabin it is difficult to know the weather or if it is light or dark outside, but inside cabins are excellent for late sleepers. As the category goes from a lower to a higher location on the ship, the price will also increase. An exception to this may be the higher up, partially obstructed or totally obstructed views from cabins. An outside ocean view cabin will be slightly higher in price, but we advise you to select an outside for your very first cruise.

In the interest of economy, a high level cabin selection is not always necessary. A medium to lower level is sufficient and you can easily reach ship facilities by stairs or elevator. If you are physically able, it is a good practice to use the stairs as often as possible for the exercise. Besides, you need to work off those extra calories the fine gourmet food brings. It seems after three or four days at sea, "that darn salt air shrinks your clothes." If you have difficulty walking, you should select a cabin near the elevators.

If the price is relatively high for a balcony/veranda, only consider it for a cruise through the Panama Canal, Alaska, New England/Canada or similar great outdoor views. Otherwise, it may not be worth the extra money. If you are an ocean lover, you may appreciate a balcony for the sights, smells and sounds of the open sea. Remember, there are many places throughout the ship to view outside. It is sometimes a challenge to determine which side of the ship to select for your balcony --port or starboard. More often than not, it doesn't matter.

When you review the brochures for layout of the ship, be sure to look carefully at the decks you are considering for a cabin. If you are considering a deck with an outside ocean view, carefully inspect the deck pictured in the brochure to see how it is structured.

The brochures are well diagramed so you can tell whether the cabin selected is near or beside elevators, over or under a disco, show lounge, jogging track or kitchen. Some noise can make its way from these areas at different times. Near the aft end (stern) of the ship in low deck cabins, you may occasionally feel a rumble of the engines, but normally this is not a continuing problem. Forward near the bow, some noise may be heard from the chains and anchors, but again, it is slight and only on occasion.

For first time cruisers, our recommendation is to select a cabin midway between the bow and the stern of the ship (midship) and low to midway up from the bottom of the ship. Don't skimp too much for your first cruise. If you make a bad selection it may turn you off from cruising, which would be a shame. If you are an "old salt" then go for what ever turns you on.

BEST TIME TO BOOK

It is wise, if possible, to book a cruise at least six months to a year early. You will have a better choice selecting a stateroom location and dining room accommodations. If your work demands or other factors affect your ability to schedule early, then book as soon as you can. To wait until the last minute sometimes works, but chances are better if you schedule your cruise early. If you book your own air to a port of debarkation, make airline reservations early. If you are booking your cruise close to the date of sailing, insure you make airline reservations for the appropriate dates and times to accommodate your cruise. If you book the air/sea package, this will be taken care of for you.

CRUISE EXPERIENCE

The goal of the family vacation is to find the experience that allows both parents and children to enjoy their favorite activities as well as spend quality time together. Many times vacations with children can be difficult to satisfy all interests.

Family vacations do not necessarily need to include theme parks or compromising adult entertainment for a child's amusement. Cruising with children can be fun, exciting and educational. Parents can visit exotic locations for excellent sightseeing, and include a geography lesson for their children. Children can have their fast foods, games, swimming and movies. A cruise ship offers security as well as fun, games and educational advantages. There are programs for all age groups.

A very young child, less than two or three years of age can be demanding for parents. If you have an infant (less than three years old), you may want to wait until the child is a little older because of the time, demands and attention required for a baby. Some cruise lines recommend you wait until a child is at least three years old before taking them on a cruise. Cruise lines normally have programs for children from age of three through teenager. Ask your travel agent what is available for a particular cruise.

Take a journal along on your cruise. This is included as an item on your packing checklist at Chapter Seven. It seems that when we go on a vacation the time whizzes by and we wonder what we did. Jotting down key activities in a journal each day will help coordinate your photos and account for your precious time on vacation.

TIPS FOR HONEYMOONERS

Cruises are great for a honeymoon! Be sure your travel agent knows your wishes when booking a "honeymoon" cruise. A dinner table for two may be requested, and perhaps off in a quiet corner, if desired. Honeymooners normally do not want to join all seniors at a large table. If you desire a large table for six or eight people, request a table with other honeymooners or young couples. A few ships may not be able to place twin beds together to make-up a queen/king. If you do not want to be singled out as honeymooners, let the travel agent know. Usually, early in a cruise, ships have get-togethers for all honeymooners. Cruise ships will offer complimentary champagne, wine or other goodies.

Many times the planning leading up to the wedding and the actual wedding can be stressful and tiring to both bride and groom. Consider departing for a cruise on your honeymoon two or three days after the wedding day. If you depart on your wedding day or early the morning after, you may be too tired, sleepy and stressed out to enjoy the first three to five days of the cruise.

Some travel agents will tell you that planning is the key. They are partly right. Planning is very important but it's only half the key. The other half is "preparing" and there is some difference.

START PREPARING

When you begin preparing for your cruise, plan what you will wear each day and for those exciting evenings. Also, we suggest you prepare a list, especially for the ladies, on what you will wear during the formal and semiformal dinners and functions.

If you handle your own airline schedule, make airline reservations as soon as possible. Sometimes at high traffic cruise embarkation points such as Ft. Lauderdale, Miami, Vancouver or San Juan, Puerto Rico, several cruise lines could be arriving and departing close to the same time. Flight reservations must be made early to schedule your desired times. Air travel seats could be limited, especially around holidays, unless you fly to the port city a day or two early.

We suggest you make two photocopies of your passport identification page, airline ticket, driver's license and the one or two credit cards you are taking along. Take one photocopy of each with you, keeping them in a separate place, and leave one copy at home. Pack an extra set of eye glasses. Leave a copy of your itinerary and how you may be reached with family or friends. There may be a need to contact you in the event of an emergency.

YOUR OWN CRUISE MATE CARD

A convenient and classy preparation is to have business/vacation cards printed with a logo and your full name, address and phone number. Usually the last evening dinner before debarkation you will have become friends with your dinner mates and may want to remember them, perhaps correspond and sail with them later. By handing out your "Cruise Mate/Vacation Card" it saves looking for scratch paper to write down the information. Your personal business card also works. It is impressive to have your own *Cruise Mate* Card". You will probably make additional friends as well and may want to exchange addresses with them. A box of cards is fairly inexpensive and can be used anytime. Leave space on the card to write in the name of the ship, route (such as Western Caribbean or Panama Canal or vacation spot) and the dates of sailing or other travels. Here is an example:

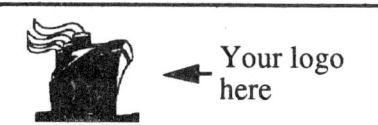

```
┌─────────────────────────────────────────┐
│                                         │
│              🚢    ← Your logo          │
│                      here               │
│  (Leave space here to write in name of  │
│  ship, where cruised and dates of cruise)│
│                                         │
│     Your Name, Address and Telephone    │
└─────────────────────────────────────────┘
```

MOTION SICKNESS

As a rule, the higher on the ship the less smooth the cruise will be in rougher seas because you are farther from the ship's center of gravity. For those who fear sea/motion sickness select a cabin towards the center of the ship near the lower level and at outside mid ship. This location tends to have less motion and allows you to look at the horizon for reference. Try to keep your mind off the ailment (easy for you to say?). Go to an outside deck for fresh air and an orientation with the horizon. Normally, it is best not to lie down. There are several preventatives or so-called aids which can be purchased over the counter. Check with your doctor. Sucking on a orange or lemon may help. Ginger, such as in Gingerale or ginger snaps sometimes help. Don't ask why...

Modern ships have lateral, gyroscopically operated stabilizers which extend out from both port and starboard sides. This prevents nearly all roll motion, 80% or more, which could cause motion sickness. While moving, the stabilizers act and are shaped similar to the ailerons of an airplane and tilt approximately twenty degrees. If the ship starts to roll starboard (to the right), the starboard stabilizer tilts down and the port (left) stabilizer tilts up. The opposite is true with a roll to port. This helps keep the ship on an even keel. Remember, less than 3% of cruisers on large ships succumb to sea sickness --and then only for a short time.

Unless you are very susceptible to motion sickness, a cruise nowadays, especially in the Caribbean, will be smooth and motion sickness will be of little concern.

MEDICAL PREPARATIONS

As far as inoculations and vaccinations are concerned, it is best for you to contact your local doctor or health service for specific information to particular areas of the world. Normally, throughout the Caribbean and most areas close to the United States, special inoculations or vaccinations may not be required. Discuss this with your travel agent.

If you are susceptible to motion sickness, consider visiting your personal doctor prior to sailing for a prescription or a recommended over the counter medication. Ships have medical facilities on board that issue motion sickness medication, some are free. There will be a doctor on the ship, but normally not a dentist. When on board, check the office hours when the doctor is available. If you need to see the doctor or nurse during other than normal office hours, an emergency fee may be tacked on to your bill. Be sure to keep all medical receipts. Review your medical plans and insurance coverage before you take a cruise.

If possible, take all current medical supplies in their original containers showing the prescription. If known, take along the generic name of a drug. This assists a doctor in handling your medical problem should it occur while on the cruise.

COMMUNICATIONS

Ship-to-shore communications are available on board the ships. Your phone calls will be billed to your ship account.

Be sure you understand that the charge per minute for such calls is very expensive. For economical reasons, it is recommended that if you want to make a phone call, use the phones at various ports-of-call.

Postage and mailing services are available on board ship. Check with the Purser's desk. Some ships offer electronic mail (E-Mail). Just as E-mail on land is economical compared to telephone service, it is also lower in cost at sea. In some instances passengers may be able to send an E-mail message from a ship for a fraction of the cost of a satellite phone call, approximately $3.00 to $5.00 per message. Check with your travel agent and don't forget to bring along your E-mail addresses.

In an emergency, those at home may contact your ship by direct dialing. Refer to the brochures provided. There is a listing of the International Access Number, Ocean Region Code Number, Ship call letter and ID Number. Callers need to have the ship name, party name and the cabin number before dialing. Calls normally go through the ship's radio room. Radiograms may also be available.

TRAVEL DOCUMENTS

Travel documents required prior to a cruise are very important. Obtaining the required documentation for embarkation to the ship is strictly your responsibility. If this is not properly accomplished, you will be denied boarding.

U. S. citizens normally do not require a passport or visa for the Caribbean, Alaska, Mexico or Canada. In many cases a drivers license/picture identification *and* a birth certificate, with a raised authentication seal, will suffice. A driver's license only is not sufficient. Be sure to check with your travel agent. Some ships, such as the Marco Polo, may require a passport at all times.

Non-U.S. citizens need a passport and must check whether a visa or similar official papers are required. Visa requirements vary from one country to another and change from time to time. Check with the local embassy or consulate of the country you are to visit. It behooves you to check with your travel agent to verify current regulations.

Cruise Mate HIGHLY RECOMMENDS you have a passport in your possession when you cruise travel. Be sure to carry it with you. Do not pack it in a suitcase. Make sure your current passport has not expired. Certain areas may require your passport not expire for six months after your return date. An application for a U.S. passport can be picked up at certain U.S. Postal Service Buildings. An adult passport is normally good for ten years. Children passports are good for five years. Apply for a passport early. It takes time to process and receive it depending on the time of year you apply. The vacation months normally take longer. Plan ahead!

CAR USE

Parking lots are available at, or close to, the areas of embarkation. The costs vary from $6.00 to $8.00 per day. Some locations, such as New York City, will charge a higher parking fee. This could be $15.00 or so per day. If you plan to take a cruise longer than seven days, consider parking elsewhere and take a taxi, shuttle or ask someone to take you to the dock. If you are from out of town and are spending two or more days in the embarkation city, a rental car is a good option. Plan to pick-up the car when you arrive and return it just before embarkation. With the popularity of cruising, a few rental car companies such as Hertz and Avis, plus a few others, will take you to the dock when you return the car.

TRAVEL SENSE

There are some things you can plan for and it is only natural to make the very most of your vacation time. Every moment of your leisure time is precious. Be sure to get trip details in writing, including any restrictions, cancellation penalties and specific costs, such as taxes or port charges. Learn about the places you are to visit. Familiarize yourself with local laws and customs in those areas. Consult your library and travel agent. Study the weather, places to avoid, best buys and interesting areas. Be familiar with the port stops so you will know what tours you may want to take. For a family of three or four it can become expensive to take a tour at each port so be selective.

In preparing, consider happenings that are not planned. Too little sun, late planes, delayed or lost luggage, large crowds, sickness, the cancelation of a scheduled port visit due to weather, labor or ship difficulties --all the annoying vacation spoilers you can't control. Maybe you cannot plan for the unexpected, but you can prepare. That is the other half of the key to a great cruise vacation. Prepare by using the following four travel senses:

Sense of Purpose

Be sure you have a sense of purpose for your cruise. You will be surprised how much time people waste because they have not figured out what they are looking for in a cruise and the tours that are available. If you want to lie by the pool or on the beach periodically during the cruise, then so be it. The important thing is to know and prepare to satisfy the purpose of your cruise.

Sense of Direction

Knowing what direction you are going is very important. Get to know the layout of the ship. Nobody enjoys being lost. It wastes time and it is terribly frustrating. It will take the first two or three days aboard ship to get oriented and find your way around. Refer to Chapter Eight for a guide on how to quickly find your way around the ship. Ports that are visited could be strange to you. Prepare for your visit. Consult the cruise line brochures, ship's tour desk and use available maps. Plan your outings at unfamiliar ports, and if necessary, swallow your pride and ask someone for direction.

Sense of Humor

Your sense of humor may be most challenged during traveling. This is especially true with lost luggage or if your responsibilities happen to involve young children. There may be little to laugh about at times, but it is recommended over crying. The airline and cruise world have unexpected gliches too. Although the ship's staff tries very hard, everything as far as service and activities may not seem to cater completely to you all the time, but adjust, keep a happy face and have a positive attitude. It will do wonders for yourself and the people around you. After all, you have taken your precious time and money to enjoy the cruise. Do not jeopardize your time by continually complaining or feeling sorry for yourself. A negative attitude and an inability to relax, results in a stressed vacation. Everything is not going to be perfect. Cruises are meant to provide new and different experiences, *but they can only happen with your permission.* Look for the positive aspects of every situation and you will find them. Remember, there could be a communication breakdown between you and the other person. There is a old saying that typifies the attitude you should take when confronted. It goes like this:

"Give me the strength and perseverance to change the things I can change, understanding and patience for the things I cannot change, and the wisdom to know the difference."

Travel-related services can be trying at times. Cruising takes most of your problems away by supplying all you will need: a comfortable place to sleep, excellent food, sight seeing, activities, great entertainment ...and it even gets better!

Common Sense

There is no substitute for common sense. Using your head and gut feeling is the number one prerequisite for successful travel. As with any foreign travel, you might visit areas that potentially could be threatening. Dress modestly and not revealing. Do not entice locals to want something you have. Ask permission before taking pictures of local people. Observe and obey local customs. Protect your valuables and be cautious of wearing flashy jewelry or displaying money. Walk on the inside of sidewalks and carry your handbag in a secure manner carrying it on the side away from the street. Avoid eye contact with strangers. Ask questions and checkout taxis or tour guides if you schedule your own shore excursions. Be aware of travel advisories. The Department of State tries to alert American travelers to adverse conditions abroad. Check with your travel agent also. It does not matter how you exercise the other three senses, if you do not use this one, you are unprepared and could be headed for trouble!

CHAPTER THREE

TRAVEL AGENT ASSOCIATION

SELECTING A TRAVEL AGENT

The careful selection of a travel agent can save you time, effort, money and even grief. Travel agents provide valuable service and counseling. The price of a cruise can vary from one travel agent to another. Cabins can vary greatly in price among fellow passengers who book similar cabins. Prices can be somewhat lower if a travel agency is promoting group rates, or the cruise line has offered regional promotions. Commissions can also vary. Prices for cruises can range from a 5% discount to 50%, or sometimes advertised as "two-for-one."

The prices published in brochures can be discounted considerably by a good travel agent using specials offered. Rarely would you have to pay the brochure prices by cruise lines. Compare per diem rate as well as total price of several ships.

Shop around. It is worthwhile to visit or contact two or three travel agents before you decide to book your cruise. Find an experienced, service-oriented travel agent. Get to know the agent and have him or her get to know you, your desires, expectations, preferences, lifestyle and budget. A good travel agent is a valuable asset and must be more than just an order-taker or ticket agent. After you have carefully reviewed a cruise brochure and discussed the cruise fully with your travel agent, only then should you place your deposit. A well informed, conscientious travel agent who carefully advises you is worth his/her weight in gold!

The next time you are out and about, stop by a travel agent's office and discuss cruising. The agent will provide you with beautiful brochures and basic information concerning various cruise lines, ship layout, sailing dates, itineraries and listed costs. Experienced agents are very good at recommending cruise lines and ships as they receive feedback from their customers (referrals). On your first visit, pick up several copies of the various cruise line brochures and take them home with you to review. On subsequent visits, discuss details such as sailing dates, destinations, ship deck plans, ship activities, price comparisons, individual needs to determine "which cruise is right for you."

Your travel agent needs to know the purpose of your cruise. Is it a romantic get away, honeymoon, family cruise, celebration, first time cruise or group get-together? Do you prefer very casual, elegantly casual, semiformal or formal surroundings? Discuss with the travel agent your expectations, lifestyle, ambiance and experience you intend to have aboard ship. Based on the information you provide, it will make a difference in the cruise line, ship and cabin location suggested by the travel agent. Remember, there are cruises for everyone: for active adults, for singles, for honeymooners, young adults, adventurers, families, seniors, physically challenged and to destinations all over the world.

Travel agents have a great responsibility to you as a customer and their services are free unless specified in print or otherwise posted. Check with the travel agent to see whether there is a fee should you have to cancel. Some travel agents charge for cancellations. Usually the fee can be applied to another cruise with that travel agent. Their knowledge can help you considerably if they are properly informed. Agents should be familiar with most of the major ships people ask about. They are periodically invited aboard various ships, sometimes for just an inspection at dock-side and a possible lunch or perhaps for a short cruise. As a minimum, the agent should have sailed on or toured some of the more popular ships. Ask them what ships they have sailed on or visited and how many cruises they book in a month. Make sure all "promises" are in writing. If the travel agent has never been on a cruise or a ship, he or she lacks first hand knowledge and may not be the travel agent to work with.

There are several types of travel agencies. Some travel agencies do "cruise-only" travel and provide a distant 800 number. Some may have a local office. Discounts can be considerable when agencies purchase large blocks of cabins. Before you contact a cruise-only agent by phone it is advisable to review all the information available so it will be easier to make a decision. Have a good understanding of the category, location, approximate date and type of cabin you would like. Long distance cruise only travel agents can be of some help in your decision making, but do not offer the more personal face-to-face service of a local office.

The "full service" travel agents who handle all types of corporate travel, cars, hotels and tours may not be as well versed in cruise travel as "cruise only" travel agents who specialize in cruising.

Cruise travel agents located in shopping centers, at department stores, local travel offices and numerous others found in the "Yellow Pages" will personally tailor your cruise to your needs. This type of agency would be best for persons requiring considerable information on their cruise. Selecting a travel agent is similar to selecting a dentist, doctor or lawyer --by word of mouth (referrals) and other individual research. Ask for recommendations from family, friends and co-workers.

The Cruise Lines International Association (CLIA) affiliated travel agencies are a good source. Many CLIA-affiliated agencies have Accredited and Master Cruise Counsellors available on their staff. These are individuals who have successfully completed a variety of cruise training programs and have visited and/or sailed on many of the ships you may be interested in. Once you find a travel agent who works well with you, keeps you informed and delivers a good value, it is advisable to stay with that agency.

Beware of scams. If you are solicited by telephone or through the mail by a marketing phrase like: "You have been selected for an exciting, inexpensive cruise with all of the amenities", be very leery, especially if you are asked for a credit card number or asked to send a check. If an offer seems too good to be true, it probably is. Check it out. You pick the travel agent, do not let the travel agent pick you.

You can verify a good agent by several methods. Better Business Bureau, company name and standing or you can check with the cruise line Customer Relations Office and ask if they do business with that agent. Try to compare one agent's suggestions, recommendations and prices with other knowledgeable sources. You can check an agency through organizations such as the American Society of Travel Agents (ASTA); the Association of Retail Travel Agents (ARTA); and the National Association of Cruise-Only Agencies

(NACOA). Certain travel magazines advertise travel agencies also.

Local travel agents will normally give a more detailed and personal service with the desire to keep you as a customer. You should always work through a travel agent for a cruise. They can usually provide you with better service, protection and prices. Once your travel agent has contacted the cruise line office, any other contacts should be made through your travel agent. The cruise line office does not want to come between you and the travel agent. The travel agent acts for you in making the cruise arrangements, including your deposit, final payment, distributing your cruise packet and advising.

After you have selected a cruise line and ship, be sure to discuss with the travel agent his/her policies and the general information contained near the back cover of the cruise line brochure prior to booking. It is *very important* you understand the pertinent conditions.

THE BOOKING

After you have reviewed the brochures and are somewhat familiar with two or three cruise lines or ships, go to the travel agent's office and discuss the possibilities with him/her. Make a list of questions you would like answered or have explained. If this is not your first cruise and you would like to try another cruise line, the travel agent should be able to supply information for a comparison. Do not overwhelm yourself with too many options.

For best results, the travel agent should be able to call the cruise line right on the spot and ask questions or make reservations. The agent must be able to price the two or three possibilities you present. Get a price with, and without, air travel. If during the first visit with the travel agent you are not sure what to do, leave, go home, think it over and discuss it with whomever you are planning to travel with. Before you decide to have the travel agent call for a booking, there are several questions you and the travel agent must work out and answer together, such as:

1. What date, length of cruise, destination(s) and lifestyle do you desire?
2. What cruise line and ship will best satisfy the date, length of cruise, destination(s) and your desired lifestyle?
3. Do you desire more casual, semiformal or formal atmosphere (dress)?
4. Are you a past passenger for that cruise line?
5. What price range are you looking for?
6. What category and type cabin do you want, inside, outside (ocean view), balcony?
7. What size ship (small, medium or large)?

8. Do you want to request an early or late seating for dinner (based on availability)? Usually parents with children select the early/main dinner seating.
9. Do you want to request a small or large dinner table (based on availability)? A small table could be a seating for two or four. A large table could be a seating for six, eight or ten.
10. Smoking or non smoking?
11. Do you have special diet needs?
12. What facilities do you require, physically challenged, if applicable?
13. Are you celebrating a birthday, anniversary, honeymoon or other special occasion?
14. Information on air/sea packages versus separate air fares.
15. What is the cruise cancellation policy? (Important!)
16. Will you need Cancellation Protection Insurance? If you might have a medical emergency, family or health related problem that could prevent you from taking the cruise, it is advisable to purchase protection insurance. This is an individual decision.
17. Does the ship take personal checks, credit cards?

If you require modified accommodations for physically challenged, oxygen or vision impaired you need to discuss this with your travel agent at the time of booking.

When you ask questions, be sure to understand the answers. Take notes and repeat back instructions and conditions. Share your thoughts and concerns. If the travel agent does not have all the answers, he/she knows where to go to satisfy your concerns. It helps to take someone along with you to the travel agent's office. If you are considering an outside cabin, ask your travel agent if the cabin has a large picture window, a porthole, partially obstructed or an obstructed view. After you decide on the booking, you can bind the contract with a deposit or you can wait a few days, usually up to seven, to think it over before you make the deposit.

The reputable cruise lines will do all they can to provide a good cruise and keep you as a repeat customer. The travel agent usually will get a better price if you are a repeat customer. Always advise the travel agent if you are a repeat customer to the cruise line you are booking with to receive a discount rate. As a repeat customer on board ship you will receive an invitation to a complementary cocktail party. The Captain, accompanied by the Cruise Director, will introduce key officers and present current information and future plans concerning the cruise line. Also awards are sometimes presented to frequent cruisers of that line.

DEPOSIT

The deposit for a written and confirmed booking could vary from $250 to $500 or more per person depending on destinations and the duration of the cruise. Cancellation periods and fees vary from cruise line to cruise line. It is extremely important to discuss with your travel agent, and thoroughly understand, cancellation policies.

Cruise lines have firm procedures when booking a cruise. They need to have a projected number of passengers to properly accommodate the cruise. If this figure continually changes after the last 60 or so days prior to sailing date, it could affect the efficiency of the cruise. Therefore, book your cruise at least six months to a year in advance when possible. This will save you money and you will be able to be selective on your cabin and its location.

As a general idea, the following chart gives an example of cancellation fees. It is best to check with your travel agent. Prepayments or deposits for most cruises and tour packages may be partially or entirely forfeited if you cancel your cruise within a *certain number of days* before departure.

TRAVEL AGENT ASSOCIATION

(Example only)

Days Prior to Sailing Date	**Charges Per Person
*60 to 90	May receive full refund. Varies with cruise line, type & length of cruise.
*59 - 30	A % charge. May lose all deposit plus more.
*29 - 7	A much larger % charge (Could be no refund).

Less than 7 days, Possibly no refund.

*Approximate days. *Check with travel agent! These days vary with each cruise line and cruise. Extended or holiday sailings may use 90 days.*
**Per person, double occupancy.

The deposit constitutes a contract. The travel agent is the agent for the passenger, therefore the passenger remains liable to the cruise line for the cost of the cruise. Some travel agents may retain part of your deposit if you cancel. Review your printed itinerary or passenger contract before you sign. As discussed previously, the deposit will vary according to the price and length of the cruise. If not included, there are also port charges and taxes to be added to your contract payment. Find out the exact cost of the cruise, understand the air transportation procedures (if selected), know when your final payment is due and the exact date that you can cancel without penalty. This will save you money and possible problems later.

CANCELLATIONS

Once you make the deposit, you are bound by the conditions for cancellation. Be sure you know how to comply with booking and contract requirements and understand the cancellation penalties. You will receive a confirmation number and either a printed itinerary or a passenger contract. You will be advised by your travel agent as to when you can cancel without penalty. Any refunds are normally credited/returned to your credit card account within 30 to 45 days. You can make a telephone call to cancel; however, under certain conditions you may need to notify in writing that you are canceling the cruise.

Discuss cancellation policies with your travel agent prior to booking because various cruises dictate different times to cancel. Holiday cruises may require 90 days or more notice for full refund. Refer to the back pages of the cruise brochure. *Be sure to understand the cancellation policies before you book!*

TRAVEL PACKET

Once you have booked your cruise and made the final payment, approximately two to three weeks before sailing, you will receive the travel packet. It is exciting to receive and it contains all necessary travel documents. The packet is either picked up at the travel agent's office or sent by express mail. If you need to check on delivery time of the packet, do so with your travel agent. Cruise line Passenger Relations will not give out information on your travel due to privacy reasons. Arrange for someone to sign for the documents when they are sent by express mail.. Review the packet thoroughly to insure you have received everything and the correct names and reservations are stated. Verify the spelling of the names. If not correct, be sure to notify your travel agent immediately.

The packet will contain forms to be filled out. These forms consist of registering on the ship for that particular sailing date. Other forms may deal with immigration and visits to other countries and islands. Be sure to fill out all forms and sign them as appropriate BEFORE you arrive at the ship for embarkation. The cruise line will also include a small brochure describing the itinerary ports of call and shore excursions with prices, duration and level of difficulty, if any. An excursion may consist of a bus ride, considerable walking or climbing. The tours are normally operated by independent vendors on shore. Regardless, if you experience any problems or difficulties, be sure and notify the Excursion Desk on board ship.

Also contained in the packet are tags you will attach to your luggage. This will address the luggage to your assigned cabin. Print your stateroom number in large, bold characters on the tags so they can easily be seen. A felt tip pen is good for this. Write your name, sailing date and any other requested information. We suggest, if you make your own flight reservations, do not attach your ship's luggage tags until after you claim your luggage from the airline at destination. If you have the air/sea package then do as the cruise line or travel agent requests.

INSURANCE

A Cruise Protection Plan (insurance) may be purchased in case of possible illness or health problems. Buying travel insurance is a way to guarantee your vacation dollars will not be lost through uncontrolled events. The protection plan normally covers trip cancellation and interruption protection, travel and baggage delays or loses, some medical expenses and emergency assistance. The insurance could cost between five and eight percent of the cruise price. Protection insurance can also be purchased from commercial companies not associated with the cruise line. There are several agencies from which to choose. If you are unsure you will be able to make the cruise, it is important to consider insurance coverage at the time of booking. It must be selected by final payment. Find out about pre-existing health conditions or injuries. *Be sure to understand what coverage you will have, what are the restrictions and how you must comply!* Read the small print in the insurance policy for exclusions. For cancellations close to the day of the cruise, less than 72 to 24 hours, a late cancelation notice may not be covered. It is best to discuss this fully with your travel agent so you will not be faced with a financial loss.

Purchasing the insurance is entirely up to you. If your cruise is not especially expensive and if you are in good health, fairly young to middle age, able to take your cruise when you plan it and do not fear a loss could occur, then a protection plan *may* not be necessary. *Cruise Mate* leans towards purchasing insurance coverage. So if you are "on the fence" consider selecting insurance for you and your family's protection during the cruise. Discuss this with your travel agent at the time you place your deposit. If not covered by insurance, medical evacuation from a ship when your condition is acute or life threatening is very expensive. Be aware of any prior ills clauses in the policy. A cruise line may disavow any direct affiliation with the insurance plan although it can be provided for their passengers. Be selective and remember, it is strictly up to you. Consult with your travel agent.

It is important to also review your own private medical insurance before you leave on a cruise. Medicare, HMOs and others may not cover you outside your area. This includes Canadians. Out-of-providence medical insurance may only cover a fraction of the medical costs. Review your coverage prior to departing from home and ask questions if you are unclear.

LATE CONTRACT FOR A CRUISE

Cruise lines can have last minute cancellations or a few cabins may not have been booked. To recoup this lost revenue within the last 30 to 15 days or so, a cruise line may notify certain travel agents to advertise a few cabins at a reduced rate. If your vacation time is flexible you can save considerably by booking standby or checking for space the last two to four weeks; it's taking a chance. Occasionally you may get a real travel bargain by receiving an up-grade for a lower economy price. On the flip side, you could get a less desirable cabin. You will need to book your own air transportation at the late date.

Sometimes cruise lines will offer a "guaranteed rate" or a "to be assigned" (TBA). This method of booking will not assign you a cabin right away, but will guarantee you a cabin equal to, or better than, the category you select at the price you paid. Another method is what may be called a "run of the ship rate". Any cabin, inside or outside, will be assigned on availability near time of sailing. Many times these booking procedures can be purchased for less money and perhaps if you are lucky you could receive a higher category cabin for the price of a lower category. It is worthwhile to ask your travel agent about them.

CHAPTER FOUR

TYPES OF CRUISES, WHERE AND WHEN

TYPES OF CRUISES

It is fun to sail on a new ship, but there is still something to be said about older ships. They present a certain experience that makes cruising elegant and nostalgic. Holland America Line, for example, had the SS Rotterdam V (Launched in 1959, retired 1997). This ship carried nostalgia, respect, tradition, class and many memories for the cruise traveler. Many Holland America ardent cruise followers cruised on this fine lady when she sailed for the last time with Holland America. The SS Rotterdam V was purchased by Premier Cruises, updated to new safety standards, and renamed "Rembrandt."

A new ship's first official cruise is the "Maiden Voyage" and a new ship's first year sailing is "The Inaugural Season". These cruises may cost a little more, but are very exciting! Sometimes, if a cruise line is pushing for completion of a new ship and its maiden voyage, there could be final work to be completed during the maiden voyage. Work crews may complete these final touches on board during the first few cruises. It takes a couple of cruises to work out the kinks. Be prepared for some minor glitches, if they occur, on the maiden voyage. Also, cruise lines pull officers, staff and crew members from other ships to operate the new ship and although they provide good service this may be the first time they have worked together. For your first cruise, or if you cruise less than once a year, it is not recommended that you go on a shakedown cruise, first sailing after major renovations, or the "Maiden Voyage" of a new ship, but the choice is yours.

Holiday cruises are sometimes a favorite in the cruise industry. These will normally occur around Thanksgiving, Christmas and New Year's Eve. Princess Cruises has specials on their "Love Boats" around Valentines Day. These cruises draw large crowds and reservations are needed well in advance. Costs of the cruises are higher than the normal seasonal cruises, but are usually festive and exciting.

Theme cruises are a favorite among the cruise set. They are a one-of-a-kind cruise for people with special interests such as music, nature or sports. They could be Country, Jazz, Blues, Big Band, '50s and '60s, comedy, health, nature and celebrities to name a few. For the serious sports fans, there are theme cruises dedicated to nearly every sport including: professional football, baseball, hockey, basketball, motor sports, ski and volleyball plus others. These cruises not only highlight the theme, but also carry on the exciting day to day cruise activities. Norwegian Cruise Line is a theme oriented cruise line. Take along outfits to participate in the themes.

Selecting a time to cruise varies greatly with your availability and destination desires. Whether it is during the high season for cruising a particular area or the slower less expensive time, price can affect your decision. Usually the cost of a cruise varies over a "Theme Cruise", "Maiden Voyage", "Holiday Cruise", "Economy Season", "Value Season" and "Peak Season." During the summer, certain cruises are more expensive. Be aware there could be more children on board if you travel June through August, during spring break (early March through mid April) and during certain holidays. Also, ships such as Disney Magic or Wonder and three to four day cruise ships will draw more children. Parents may want to travel with children at this time while others without children may want to make another choice.

REPOSITIONING CRUISE

A repositioning cruise is a good bargain. Keep in touch with your travel agent and have the agent watch for the repositioning of ships. The itinerary is usually very good and the price is right. You can save money on such a cruise. Some cruise lines will remove their ships which have been sailing in one area and move them to another area. For example, ships could be in the Caribbean during the winter sailing the eastern, western or southern Caribbean. When it comes time for the Alaska cruises, cruise lines will reposition their ships in late April or May to get ready for the May to September Alaska season. The same holds true for New England and Canada during late summer and early fall. Cruise lines do not reposition their ships without attracting paying passengers. Sometimes these cruises are not heavily advertised and are normally longer than seven days.

Some of the cruise lines reposition their ships from the Caribbean to Bermuda, Alaska, Mexican Riviera, New England, Canada, Pacific coast and various overseas areas. The cruise lines offer itineraries year round for many different travel destinations. Ships seldom, if ever, sit idle. Be aware, and possibly prepared, that itineraries are subject to change without notice due to weather, port labor problems or unforeseen ship difficulties.

WHERE AND WHEN TO CRUISE

During late June to early November, hurricane season occasionally presents itself in the Caribbean. A few ships remain in the Caribbean during this season. However, cruise lines and officers are very cautious and safety minded. If necessary they can alter their itinerary to circumnavigate any storms which may occur.

TYPES OF CRUISES WHERE AND WHEN

No matter where you choose to cruise, you are certain to have fun. The following is a general rule of thumb, or just suggestions for destinations and recommended times of the year to cruise:

WHERE TO	WHEN
Caribbean	October to June. Family cruising late May or early June to September, weather permitting. Hurricane season is late June to November.
Alaska	Late May to late August. Sometimes overcast with occasional rain showers. Usually May and June are driest months. Starts to cool off the end of August.
Mexico	Fall, winter and spring months (summers are hot).
Panama Canal	October through May.
Bermuda	Mid May to mid October.

Hawaii	All year. During December to May good for humpback whale watching, especially around Maui.
Europe (Mediterranean)	Mostly spring to fall months (April - October). Mediterranean and southern areas are good nearly all year. The Greek Islands, Italy and countries bordering the Aegean and Mediterranean Seas become hot during the summer months. May or September are good months to cruise there.
Northern Europe	Summer (late June to mid August).
Canada - New England Northeast coast of United States.	Mid to late August to mid October (fall). Great views in early fall for autumn foliage. Rich in beauty and history, even whales.
The Baltic	Late May to early October.
The Black Sea	Late April to mid October.
Antarctica	Mid November to late January or early February Few ships are equipped to sail here.
Great Britain	Early June to early September.

TYPES OF CRUISES WHERE AND WHEN

Arctic, Iceland, Greenland areas	Late June to early August.
Scandinavia (northern countries)	Mid June through August.
South America	October to April (year-round at North Coast).
Holy Land and nearby countries	October to April.
Southeast Asia and Orient	Late October to Early April.
South Pacific	April to September (a few tropical storms in July and August). Sometimes year round can be good.

SELECTING AN ITINERARY

ALASKA

The Alaska trip will certainly offer experiences of grandeur of the great outdoors, mountains, glaciers, icebergs, salmon, bald eagles, the Humpback and Orca whales plus other mammals, and perhaps a bear or two. Alaska is beautiful and a camera cannot do it justice. It is country you must see with your own eyes. A camcorder is good to capture "calving" glaciers and beautiful landscapes. The journey through the Inside Passage is dotted with seaport villages, fjords, light houses and forested mountains. Available for your visit is a close-up look at Glacier Bay, the Mendenhall Glacier, historic gold-rush boom towns and many side adventures. The Mendenhall Glacier is one of many "rivers of ice" formed during the Little Ice Age which began about 3,000 years ago.

Cruise enthusiasts are enthralled by the beauty and awesomeness of the Inside Passage. Many will return again for a different cruise continuing north past Whitehorse and the Yukon to Anchorage docking at Seward and/or College Fjord. By cruising this route, the Inside Passage as well as the Gulf of Alaska, more glaciers may be seen. You can also make this a jump-off point to explore more of Alaska's interior. Here you can find the highest mountain in North America, Mount McKinley which reaches 20,320 feet. There are three million lakes and 34,000 miles of coastline, more than in all other states combined.

It is somewhat of a gamble on misty and wet weather and temperatures. The temperatures can range from 40s to 75 degrees. You need to take an umbrella, a rain coat/slicker, a sweater, jacket or light coat to layer clothing as needed.

In Alaska there are many side trips available. Activities include river rafting, kayaking, bicycling, flight-seeing, hiking, boat charters, aircraft sight seeing, scuba diving, skiing and even a nine hole golf course in Juneau.

CARIBBEAN

There are two pronunciations of "Caribbean." The sea takes its name from the "Carib" Indians, pronounced CARE-ib who were the predominant inhabitants when Columbus arrived in 1492. Caribs were warlike cannibals and their name comes from the Spanish word for cannibal - Caribe. Therefore you can say: Care-ih-BEE-un or Kuh-RIB-ee-yun, either is correct.

Cruise lines divide the Caribbean into several areas for their cruises. There are cruises to the Eastern Caribbean; the Southern Caribbean; the Western Caribbean; the Panama Canal turn around (round-trip); and the Panama Canal cruise that completely transits the canal. Near the tip of Florida are the Bahamas. These numerous, beautiful small islands are surrounded by radiant clear blue and green water and are great for short cruises of three or four days in duration. The Bahamas are actually located in the Atlantic Ocean.

Caribbean itineraries vary with each cruise line. Seven to twelve day cruises will normally edge through the Atlantic Ocean and the Caribbean Sea, toward the Greater Antilles near the Leeward and/or the Windward Islands and the Lesser Antilles. Departure cities for Caribbean cruises are Ft. Lauderdale, Miami, San Juan, Houston, New Orleans or Tampa Bay. Holland America, Princess, Royal Caribbean,

Disney, Costa and Norwegian Cruise Lines own or lease private islands where their ships call during seven and ten day Caribbean cruises. They invest considerable sums of money developing portions of these islands. Passengers are treated to water sports and a very nice barbecue.

EASTERN CARIBBEAN

Normally, you will cruise the Eastern Caribbean to San Juan, Puerto Rico for Spanish history, forts, Old San Juan and monuments. Goods purchased in Puerto Rico and brought into the continental U.S. have special personal custom allowances. Bargains in Puerto Rico include Bacardi Rum, mounted butterflies, carved wood, lace work, guitars, paper-mache festival masks plus others.

Visit St. Maarten for Dutch culture as the Dutch section is part of the Netherlands Antilles. St. Maarten is the smallest territory in the world governed by two sovereign states, Dutch (St. Maarten) and French (St Martin). English, French and Dutch are spoken there. The word Antilles means "island" and comes from the legendary island of Antilia which was thought to lie between Europe and Asia. Supposedly, this was the refuge of Christians fleeing Spain when the Moors invaded. The larger islands: Cuba, Jamaica, Hispaniola and Puerto Rico are called the Greater Antilles. The smaller islands, which form the east border of the Caribbean spanning the distance from Puerto Rico to the tip of South America, are the Lesser Antilles.

St. Lucia, resembles an island in the South Pacific. It is a volcanic isle, with mountains, scenery, rugged green jungle, rolling farmland, beaches with both white and black sand and a quaint fishing village. English and French are the main languages; visit St. Thomas, U.S. Virgin Islands for excellent duty-free shopping and fine beaches. Near St. Thomas is St. John, the smallest of the U.S. Virgin Islands. Two-thirds of St. John is a national park which contains unspoiled tropical beauty. Very worthwhile to visit. There is St. Barts (Barthelemy), home of the rich and famous, and mainly French is spoken. Antiqua (pronounced 'Antiga'), has statues of John the Divine and John The Baptist which stand beside the gates of Saint John's Cathedral. It is said that these statues came from one of Napoleon's ships. English is the language. You can also visit Dominica, St. Croix, the largest of the U.S. Virgin Islands, St. Kitts, and more...

WESTERN CARIBBEAN

The Western Caribbean has excellent shopping and beaches as well. Stops include Key West, Florida with its colorful history. Ernest Hemingway lived and wrote there (1927-1938) and it was a favorite vacation island for President Truman. Visit Grand Cayman with the Seven Mile beach, soft sands and snorkeling, swim with the stingrays and turtles, sail, wind surf and dive in a submarine. Grand

Cayman also has duty-free shopping bargains such as bone china, perfume and cosmetics, crystal, caymanite jewelry, English linen and wool, rum and rum cakes. The Cayman Islands have no sales tax, but their dollar is worth approximately $1.25 U.S.

Cozumel contains the history of the Mayan kings and archaeological sites as well as extensive Mexican bargains. Jamaica has plantations and you can climb the Dunn's River Falls. Jamaica was a pirate stronghold of Port Royal and was governed by the infamous Henry Morgan who would attack Spanish ships and brutally abuse prisoners. Half of Port Royal slid into the harbor during a 1692 earthquake. Haiti and the Dominican Republic (Spanish) are nice to visit with some duty-free shops, and many other ports.

SOUTHERN CARIBBEAN

The Southern Caribbean cruise may extend to Martinique, French; St. Lucia, English and French; also, the Lesser Antilles; "ABC" Islands of Aruba, Bonaire and Curacao, whose languages vary from English, French and Dutch to Papiamento. Papiamento is a language mixture of Dutch, Spanish, Portuguese, English, French and literally means "to talk." Aruba is a Dutch tropical jewel with a floating market, beaches (on the leeward side) with snorkeling, rides on glass bottom boats and submarines.

Visit Barbados for British flavor, restored sugar plantations and classic sand beaches. Also, the statue of Admiral Lord Nelson in Trafalgar Square predates the one in London's Trafalgar Square by twenty-seven years. The island of Grenada, also English, has a parliamentary government and lies at the southern end of the Windward Islands.

English is the predominant language in the republic of Trinidad and Tobago. It is interesting to note that petroleum, among other products, forms the basis of their economy. Crude oil is produced in southern Trinidad, mainly offshore. It is said that the steel drum as a musical instrument originated on these islands because of the crude oil drum containers. Some of the preceding islands are located a small distance north of Venezuela.

Guadeloupe (primarily French) is made up of two islands and formed like a butterfly with tropical rain forests, fields of sugarcane and even a smoldering volcano. Cruises to the Southern Caribbean can sail from the Continental United States (CONUS) or San Juan, Puerto Rico. Usually, the Southern Caribbean cruise from the CONUS is longer than seven days; however there are some for seven days out of San Juan.

The Caribbean is excellent for everyone from children to adults and the young at heart. There is much to do in the towns, mountains and parks, as well as swimming in the beautiful turquoise water that washes gently on the beaches --and lots of sunshine to enjoy it all. You can snorkel, scuba dive, wade, swim or just lay on the beautiful sandy beaches. The Caribbean is a good place to start cruising, especially in the winter.

BERMUDA

Bermuda lies much to the north of the islands of the Caribbean. It is situated near the same latitude as North Carolina. Bermuda is a colorful island with traditional British charm. There is the city of Hamilton and town of St. George, from King's Wharf to the pink sand of Southhampton's many beaches. Shopping is one of the most enjoyable pastimes in Bermuda, but price haggling is not their markets' style. Many stores tend to be more sophisticated. Bermuda typically imports European products which include British woolens and cashmeres, Scottish tartans and Irish linens. They also carry crystal, porcelain, jewelry, watches, fragrances, figurines and other interesting items that you just can't live without.

Bermuda has a mild climate most year round. It boasts dramatic pink beaches, sparkling waters and lots of beautiful flowers. The traffic on the island is slight as automobile numbers are controlled. There are no rental cars, but scooters or mopeds can be rented, if you dare. You can hire a taxi or take a bus. There are certain British customs that must be adhered to such as your mode of dress away from the beaches. Bermuda has no income tax, no illiteracy and almost no unemployment.

NEW ENGLAND AND CANADA

Take a cruise journey to renowned places on the East Coast of the U.S. and Eastern Canada for captivating beauty and fascinating history. You can discover them as they were first discovered by sea, years ago. Sailing between New York and Montreal, Canada during the legendary fall colors is indescribable. Montreal is a city within a city both on the surface and underground. There is the Cathedral of Reine-Du-Monde a replica of St. Peter's in Rome and the Basilica of Notre Dame. Northward to Quebec City, the walled city, is the landmark of Chateau Frontenac, built by the Canadian Union Pacific Railroad and a summit meeting place which included President Roosevelt during World War II. The cruise on Saguenay Bay presents a fjord that is captivating and you may even see some playful whales. On to Halifax, Nova Scotia and Bar Harbor, Maine for some fresh lobster, depending on the ship's itinerary. Like Alaska, the Canada/New England cruise is something you should see with your own eyes. The Eastern Seaboard architecture and culture is breathtaking.

PANAMA CANAL

In 1534, Charles I of Spain ordered the first survey of a proposed canal route through the Isthmus of Panama, but nothing became of it. Over three centuries passed before the first construction was started by the French in 1880. The French labored twenty years, but disease, lack of proper equipment and financial problems defeated them. Then, in 1903 the United States undertook the task. The U.S. purchased the rights from the defunct French Canal Company for $40 million and completed the monumental project in ten years, ahead of schedule, at a cost of approximately $387 million.

A cruise through the Panama Canal is exciting and the total cruise time can take ten days or more. The canal is approximately 51 miles long from deep water in the Atlantic to deep water in the Pacific. It takes eight to ten hours to completely transit the canal. A ship is raised and lowered 85 feet to accomplish the crossing. The canal runs from northwest to southeast. The original elevation was 312 feet above sea level where it crosses the Continental Divide in the rugged mountain range. The Atlantic Ocean has a small tide of approximately eight inches while the Pacific Ocean has a tide between 21 and 23 feet.

To give you an idea of the dirt and rocks removed from the Panama Canal, the following example is illustrated. If the Great wall of China was moved to the United States it would reach from San Francisco to St. Louis (approximately). However, the rock and dirt taken from the excavation of the Panama Canal would build a wall as high and thick as the wall from San Francisco to New York.

The maximum allowable dimensions for regular transits of the canal are:

   Ship's beam 32.3 meters
           Approximately 106 feet

   Ship's length 294.1 meters
           Approximately 964.9 feet

   Ship's draft 12 meters
           Approximately 39 feet

Based on this, some of the new mega-ships cannot pass through the canal locks and are mainly kept in the Atlantic areas. Unfortunately, modern Navy aircraft carriers and many supertankers cannot fit through the Panama locks either. It is quite possible some commercial shippers find it just as cost effective to off-load cargo on the east or west coast and ship by rail to the other coast to be reloaded on another ship.

Although wider than the Panama Isthmus, perhaps a look could be taken at the Republic of Nicaragua for a new larger and more accommodating canal. Would it be possible the cut could be along the San Juan River to Lake Nicaragua from the Caribbean to the Pacific Ocean? (Well,...it's a thought.) Lake Nicaragua was once a bay of the Pacific Ocean.

Excellent narrations accompany the passage through the Panama Canal. This is a good history lesson for teenagers and adults alike. There are many stops along the way from Pacific to Atlantic, and Atlantic to Pacific, that make this cruise one of the very best. During a Panama Canal cruise the Mexican Riviera is beautiful for the country, weather, beaches, excellent bargains and fascinating history. Do not overlook this cruise.

OVERSEAS

There are many overseas areas where cruises can be taken. By reviewing the brochures provided by your travel agent or the cruise lines, many areas can be considered as possibilities. When you start scheduling cruises across the Atlantic or Pacific, the cost will mount up considerably. Fuel, food stuffs and other support requirements are generally more expensive to the cruise lines overseas. For the average person with average means it may be a question of whether you want to take one long cruise overseas or a couple of seven or ten day cruises near North America for about the same price. For the beginner, a seven day cruise will fit the bill very well.

Remember, a cruise is an exciting journey and a wonderful process, so enjoy every minute in your own way. Any way you do it, a cruise to anywhere in the world is great!

CHAPTER FIVE

SELECTING A CRUISE LINE AND SHIP

CRUISE SHIP PRICING

There are many cruise lines that deserve attention in the standard, premium and luxury classifications and price ranges which give the cruise traveler a great cruise for the money. As a general rule, you get what you pay for. We are unable to cover all ships in *Cruise Mate*, but will focus attention on what we consider the more popular cruise lines and ships most Americans and Canadians have easy access.

There are well over 250 ships in the cruise business and the only way *Cruise Mate* can give helpful advice on the selection of a cruise line and ship is to discuss the popular ships from mid-priced (standard to premium) through higher priced luxury ships. For international ratings these ships rate from three or four star to a five or six star. Usually the five star plus level is more expensive. Be aware there are many more to choose from. Some examples are Commodore Cruise Line with their Enchanted Capri and

Enchanted Isle sailing out of New Orleans and the smaller "Coastal Cruise Ships" which sail to lesser known areas in and near United States waters as well as around Europe and other countries.

Ship layout is graphically shown in the cruise line brochures obtained from your travel agent or cruise lines. The brochure price by category can be compared from one ship to another and from one cruise line to another. This price is usually fictional and a good travel agent will contract for less. Also a good comparison can be made with the listed per diem rate of each ship which can range from approximately $130 per day to over $800 per day per person.

When looking at a particular cruise you will notice the price is adjusted according to seasons and type of cruise. The cruise price will vary from a lower price at repositioning cruise and economy season to a higher price at peak season or for a special cruise time, such as Christmas or New Year. If you select a cabin at the lower levels of the ship forward or aft it will also save you money.

Cruise lines, among other reasons, will price their ships according to destinations, category, time of year, length of cruise, new ship and old. Cruises to Alaska during the summer and to New England/Canada during the fall are usually more expensive because of short seasons and demand. The fares of older ships, in some instances, may not be the same as those of the newer ones; although the older ships provide an excellent cruise experience. There are cruise vacations to suit every budget.

CRUISE SHIP SIZE

Cruise ships come in various sizes and passenger carrying capabilities. A small ship could carry up to 500 passengers. A midsize ship can carry from 500 to 1,000 passengers and a large ship normally carries from 1,000 to 2,000 passengers. Then, of course, there are the mega-ships currently being launched that can carry well over 2,000. Some mega-ships carry over 3,000 passengers. Selecting a ship size will have a bearing on how you will fit into the lifestyle of the ship. THIS IS IMPORTANT.

Passenger flow and the passenger space ratio determines how spacious or dense a ship may be. Some mega-ships, such as the Grand Princess, have a nice passenger flow so a crowded condition is not noticed or even a problem. The effectiveness of management with handling passenger embarkation, debarkation, tendering and even buffets is more important than size of the ship during these activities.

Medium through mega-ships offer varied and continuous activity programs throughout the day. At first, you may have some frustration finding your way around a large ship

(*Cruise Mate* will help you, refer to Chapter Eight). Small ships have a small culinary advantage that possibly allows dishes to be cooked more to order. They are like a small town, or even a small hotel, you will get to know some of the people a little better. No matter what size ship you choose, it is important to find out if you will feel at home among the ship's normal clientele and dress.

The more people on board (to a point) the more diversity you can expect of age, background and education. Normally, the less expensive the cruise, the more diverse the passengers will be. Singles are usually better off cruising on a large ship. There are more likely to be other singles whom they can have fun with at the disco and singles get-togethers. The ship's safety is great for singles. A lady can feel safe during late hours at all activities. As the cruise cost exceeds the middle priced cruises, the more semiformal to formal a cruise becomes and the clientele can expect a more formal lifestyle.

WHERE SHIPS ARE BUILT

Nearly all ships are built overseas where designers and workers are well trained and well experienced. Some of the major shipyards are located in Germany, Italy, Finland, France and Poland plus a few other areas.

OVERVIEW OF MID PRICE SHIPS

The following cruise lines vary somewhere along the mid price range, that is, from "standard" through "premium." As a result of direct experience and according to passengers interviewed who have sailed on various ships with these cruise lines, there is a consensus of opinion that they give passengers excellent cruise values. Again, each and every ship is different, even within the same cruise line. These lines come recommended and sail very nice ships.

American Hawaii Cruises
Carnival Cruise Lines
Celebrity Cruises
Costa Cruises
Delta Queen Steamboat Company River Cruises
Disney Cruise Line
Holland America Line
Norwegian Cruise Line
Orient Lines
Princess Cruises
Royal Caribbean International

A "THUMBNAIL SKETCH"

Celebrity, Holland America, Princess, Orient, and some Royal Caribbean ships provide more upscale, premium cruises, with few exceptions. Ship lifestyle, service, food, hotel and entertainment are rated mostly four and five star by leading travel magazines.

Partly standard, with occasional premium, are Disney, Norwegian, Costa, Carnival, and some Royal Caribbean ships. The latter lines tend to lean less toward formality and more along the lines of active family, sport, adult and casual cruises. Several Royal Caribbean ships provide a nice cross section of intrinsically casual (standard) and some upscale semiformal (premium) cruising.

Orient Lines and its ship, Marco Polo, was purchased by Norwegian Cruise Line in 1998. The Marco Polo is constructed with an ice-strengthened hull for adverse Arctic ice conditions and sails on many interesting, adventure itineraries. Norwegian has excellent sport and theme programs and also sails from the Port of Houston (sometimes called "Texaribbean" sailings). The new Disney Cruise Line vacations are ideal for families with children. Perhaps it should not be considered as a first time cruiser's choice unless it is strictly for your children; although, adult entertainment has been improved. Costa, the largest line in Europe, has a definite European flavor with an Italian flair and casualness. Caribbean cruises have more Americans and Canadians. Cruise lines positioned in Europe could have more European passengers.

SELECTING A CRUISE LINE AND SHIP

Most ships of Carnival are very casual with a theme park atmosphere. Many of the Carnival ships tend to be somewhat "glitzy" with some Las Vegas splash and may appeal more to singles and young married couples. The Carnival Cruise Line is an innovator and very successful at it's approach.

The Delta Queen Steamboat Company has authentic and nostalgic river steamboats cruising the rivers of America. American Hawaii Cruises offers Hawaiian ambience and sightseeing by sea around the Hawaiian Islands. The ship is home-docked in Honolulu.

All previous mentioned cruise lines and the luxury cruise lines are discussed in more detail later in this chapter.

WHAT'S RIGHT FOR YOU

Many cruise enthusiasts tend to be loyal to a particular cruise line. Cruise passengers will repeat a cruise line or particular ship over and over depending on which one they feel is right for them. This is one way to select, but consider the fun of experiencing an unknown. If you know exactly what the ship and itinerary are each time, it may not be as exciting as trying another ship or cruise line with different destinations, personality and perhaps lifestyle. A certain type ship typically attracts a certain type person. *There are no best ships in the world, only the ones that are best for you.* We emphasize you must select the cruise lines and ships that are right for you and are selected for the right reasons. Select a ship you will have more in common regarding lifestyle and other passengers on board. This is important in taking a major step toward a happy and satisfying cruise for you and your cruise mates. Of course, it is very difficult to completely satisfy everyone all the time, but ship's personnel try very hard to accomplish the task.

A few other lines and ships that belong to the middle or slightly lower standard price group may be a "close step" below in some rating marks, but still are fine ships and offer a good cruise. Some lines with smaller or older ships tend to be more casual in dress and activities. A cross section of young to older cruisers may be interested in such a lifestyle. However, *Cruise Mate* will not address these lines.

Taking each of the cruise lines and ships individually and discussing the overall rating of each ship is not appropriate for comparisons to help you in the selection of your cruise. The best way to compare a cruise line and ship is to first evaluate your particular needs. What is affordable, how casual, semiformal, formal for lifestyle. What destinations and your purpose for the cruise. What do you want to accomplish and experience on your cruise? How will the evening dress suit you? Each cruise ship is individual and differs in many respects. It depends on what *TOTAL* experience you anticipate that greatly assists in the selection of a particular cruise and ship. If you select a ship which is more formal than casual, be prepared to support the dress and behavior requirements. For courtesy to other passengers and the ship's staff, please do not try to change or ignore the dress code, especially in the dining room.

SHIP SELECTION

Two of the better ways to select a cruise line are a competent travel agent or word of mouth (referral). But don't discount reading a good reference book which aptly educates you on cruising--such as *Cruise Mate*. If someone you know has sailed with a particular cruise line or ship and had a great time, that person can affect your thinking. The opposite also works for unsatisfactory experiences. But in the case of a friend's adverse remarks, keep in mind the person may not have made a choice which was best for him/her. Cruisers may try a cruise line and have an excellent experience and therefore return to the same line again and again. After you have sailed with a particular cruise line (a repeater), you will be offered benefits and discounts for future cruises.

You can select a mega-ship, a cruise liner, a classic liner, a cruise yacht, a motor sail vessel, a river boat and the list goes on. For the beginner, a cruise liner (large ship) or mega-ship may be the best bet. They offer excellent samplings for sport, dining, sleeping accommodations, food and great entertainment. In this category, ships offer a casual, semiformal, formal and a combination of the three during the cruise experience.

When selecting a cruise line, cruise ship, itinerary and dates for sailing, your desired experience is the major consideration (How profound?). Some select a ship strictly for destinations. You can combine a cruise with side tours for sightseeing, shopping, horseback riding, hiking, golf, yacht sailing, sight-seeing flights, bike and even raft and barge trips. Another possible approach is to read, lie by the pool or on the beach and indulge in a quiet restful cruise. Keep in mind your sense of purpose when you select a ship.

There is no doubt the cruise lines want you as a customer and they want your return business. Many new ships have been launched or are scheduled to enter service within the near future. This creates great excitement in the cruise industry! Cruise lines are offering passengers choices. More and more people are joining the world of cruising!

Advertising by cruise lines can also have an affect on your choice. Many specials are offered especially for inside cabins, off season cruises and perhaps on older ships. Advertisements may state a seven day cruise starts at approximately $700 for an inside cabin. These cabins are nice and in most cases are similar to outside cabins. Much depends on the travelers budget and desires. Normally on three to seven day cruises, much of your time is not spent in your cabin since many activities are going on throughout the ship. Many cabins are not especially large, but comfortable.

A word of advice on your first cruise, spend just a little more and take a cruise with a reputable and proven cruise line. Your very first cruise is so important. Select this cruise carefully as you will remember it always. Choose an ocean view cabin if possible. Many times for just a few dollars more you can upgrade and have a memorable experience you will treasure for a life time. After you have cruised a couple times, you will know more about selection which will help you with future bookings.

Cruises vary in length of days. A cruise could be three, four, seven, ten, twelve, fourteen or more days in duration. For the new cruiser, you may want to take a shorter cruise of three, four or seven days to check cruising out and see whether you like it. The short cruise also accommodates the person who has limited time. Chances are once you take a cruise and have a pleasant experience, you will want to take another one soon. Normally, the three or four day cruise is too short and you will not want to leave the ship when it returns to port. (Please don't call a ship a "boat", you will insult the Captain.) Besides, you want to use the nautical terms to show others how experienced you are with sailing! (Note: *Cruise Mate* contains a glossary of nautical terms.) If you spend a considerable amount of money for your air fare, it would be wise to go on a seven day, or longer cruise; perhaps even two cruises back-to-back.

GRADING SHIPS

Certain publications and reports contain articles rating sanitation aboard various cruise lines. Cruise ships frequenting U.S. ports (more than six months out of the year) are subject to unannounced inspections within the voluntary cooperation of the cruise line. These inspections are conducted by the U.S. Public Health's "Center for Disease Control" (CDC) and Prevention. Their purpose is to check levels of sanitation that will possibly prevent gastrointestinal disease outbreaks on the cruise ships. Although the occurrence is not frequent, it can happen if crews on the ships do not strictly comply with standards of cleanliness. There are several areas inspected, but major concerns are (1) Water, (2) Food preparation and holding, (3) Possible contamination of food and (4) General cleanliness and storage.

The ship must receive a score of 86 or higher to pass. Ships usually score around 90 and higher. Very few fail. If they do score below 86, they immediately correct the situation and soon are rechecked. A score of 100 is very difficult to achieve, but over the years a few ships have done so. Many hotels and restaurants on land would find it difficult to receive a rating much above 86. The inland river boats and ships within U.S. waterways are inspected by state health sanitation departments, the Food and Drug Administration and occasionally by the U.S. Coast Guard.

Other areas evaluated: (1) Type Service; (2) Food quality and quantity; (3) Staterooms/Cabins; (4) Entertainment, Recreation; (5) Excursions (6) Destinations, Ports and (7) Ship Description, Type Facilities. These major areas break down into many subdivisions within each heading and can include: cleanliness, food specialty and presentation, general sanitation, bar service, maintenance, creature comfort areas, public area accommodations, cruise for the money and several other finer points for ratings. The results provide an overall number rating that can be compared with each cruise line and ships. Travel magazine articles should be used only as additional information and not as a major factor in making your final choice. In fact, a low or high rating will be history by the time you cruise on the ship. Good quality consistency is important. Cruise line management and shipboard officers pay particular attention to sanitation and safety.

PASSENGER AGE SCALE

For passenger age comparisons of various cruise lines, *Cruise Mate* uses the age of 50 as the median age on ships. Using 50, we will give our opinion of the percentage of passengers a cruise line carries above and below the age of 50. Gradually, more and more passengers below the age of 50 are cruising on many of the cruise lines.

There could be more seniors on longer cruises of ten or more days, depending on the season and ship, since they can cruise for a longer time. There is usually a good age mix below 50 and above 50 years of age. This mix can vary from 70% to 30% to half and half depending on dates of the cruise, destinations and the cruise ship. There are plenty of activities for the young, singles, middle age and seniors. More children, teenagers and active adults will cruise on Carnival ships, the Disney Magic and Disney Wonder.

SHIP ROOMINESS AND PASSENGER SPACE RATIO

The passenger space ratio (PSR) is one way to have an idea of spaciousness, density and elbowroom of a ship. It indicates a comfort index. This is figured by taking the gross registered tonnage (GRT) of the ship and divide it by the number of passengers. GRT is really not weight, it is space displacement on a ship and normally is the basis by which port and other dues are calculated. A ship's gross tonnage is the total displacement of permanently enclosed spaces, not counting the radio room, the bridge and other crew areas. One GRT is equal to 100 cubic feet of enclosed space displacement. The use of tonnage to measure volume dates to the 13th century when merchant ships carried wine in casks known as "tuns" which were approximately 252 gallons. Some years ago, Circa 1854, the Moorsom System devised tonnage regulations for maritime use.

For example: the Grand Princess has a gross registered tonnage of 108,806 tons with a normal, two passenger basis per cabin load of 2,600. Dividing 108,806 by 2,600 computes to a passenger space ratio of 41.8, which provides excellent passenger space. One ship's design may offer extra roomy cabins while another may emphasize larger public rooms.

Continuing in this chapter is information concerning cruise lines and ships currently in-being or planned at the printing of *Cruise Mate*. "Approximately" means that some ships are sold, retired, purchased, refitted, names changed and many new ships are launched. This varies from year to year, and even from month to month. The date next to the ship is the approximate month and year the ship was built or entered service. If there are two or more dates, they indicate updates or refurbish dates. The passenger count is the normal cruise capacity (two passengers per cabin). PSR stands for Passenger Space Ratio. The following shows how it relates:

50:1 or above is the ultimate in roominess,
40 to 49 is spacious,
30 to 39 has good passenger flow and sufficient elbow room,
Below 30 is considered high density (less space per person). With more than two passengers in several staterooms, the ship may be crowded.

The preceding information pertains to all ships listed in this chapter.

HOLLAND AMERICA LINE

"A Tradition of Excellence." The Holland America Line was founded during 1873 as the Netherlands-America Steamship Company, a shipping and passenger line. Because it provided service to the Americas, it became known as Holland America Line. Holland America is one of the oldest in the ship industry and marked its 125th year of business in 1998. Their logo depicts two ships, Holland America's MS Nieuw Amsterdam II with Henry Hudson's Explorer in front of the ship's starboard bow. The art was allegedly done in New York Harbor.

In 1872 they introduced their first flag ship, named for the city in which she was built. On October 15, 1872 this first Rotterdam sailed at 10 knots and carried 396 passengers. It took fifteen days to cross the Atlantic from the Netherlands to New York City. Holland America transported a considerable number of immigrants to the United States in the early 1900s. The Holland America Line is generally a semiformal cruise line and boasts of its four and five star fleet.

There is a special class and elegance about Holland America ships. They consist of fine art, sculptures, flower arrangements, classic furniture and a certain dignity. The cruise line offers quality, style and tradition. It is sedate, but not quite staid. Holland America has been named several years in a row "The best cruise value". Several of Holland America's executive chefs have been inducted into the prestigious "Confrerie de la Chaine des Rotisseurs international gastronomic society." The crew members are from the Philippines and Indonesia and are very good at pampering the passengers. Holland America makes that extra effort to give passengers an excellent cruise.

The line states a "no tipping required" policy and do not add 15% service charge to bar purchases. However, tipping and gratuities are accepted for good service, and service is always good on Holland America ships. *Cruise Mate* advocates tipping and gratuities commensurate with other cruise line guides (refer to Chapter Nine). The ships offer lots to do with the fun, entertainment and excitement of other cruise lines. Holland prices its cruises at the medium level with lots of benefits for its Alumni.

Normally, each Holland America ship will have a priest on board for many sailings. Cruises of ten days or longer will also have a Protestant minister. A rabbi will usually be on board for all sailings during Jewish holidays. Generally, cruises 14 days and longer will have a few gentlemen social hosts on board.

Holland America Westours has a large private motor coach company. It is one of the largest and most experienced cruise and cruise-tour operators in Alaska and Canada's Yukon.

THE WORLD OF HOLLAND AMERICA

Holland America sails to approximately twenty-three areas of the world plus Grand World Voyages. This includes Africa, South America, Central America, Mexico, Bahamas, Europe, Black Sea, India, Russia, Scandinavia, the Mediterranean, Trans-Atlantic, Australia, Indonesia, Southeast Asia, New Zealand, China, Japan, the Caribbean, Alaska, Panama Canal, Canada/New England and Hawaii.

PASSENGERS

The longer trips exceeding seven days during the winter months may see more adults above the age of 50. This could be 60% over 50 years of age versus 40% younger adults and children. Passenger ages depend on the destination and time of year. Holland America ships are nice for a fine traditional cruise experience with classy decor. The line has a strong following of repeat cruisers. There may not be many late night party-seekers or a large number of swingers at late disco. In addition to the formal night dress, passengers tend to dress semiformal for evening dinners, although there are several casual nights authorized. Holland America is a premium cruise line.

SHIPS

Holland America has approximately eleven ships. This number varies from year to year.

1. MS Nieuw Amsterdam, July 1983
   1,214 passengers, 33,930 tons
   PSR 27.9

2. MS Noordam, April 1984
   1,214 passengers, 33,930 tons
   PSR 27.9

3. MS Westerdam, May 1986/88, March 1990 1,494 passengers, 53,872 tons
   PSR 36.0

4. MS Statendam, January 1993
   1,266 passengers, 55,451 tons
   PSR 43.8

5. MS Maasdam, December 1993
   1,266 passengers, 55,451 tons
   PSR 43.8

6. MS Ryndam, October 1994
   1,266 passengers, 55,451 tons
   PSR 43.8

7. MS Veendam, May 1996
   1,266 passengers, 55,451 tons
   PSR 43.8

8. MS Rotterdam VI
   1,316 passengers, November 1997
   60,000 tons, PSR 45.5

9. MS Volendam, August 1999
   1,440 passengers, 63,000 tons
   PSR 43.7

10. MS Zaandam, February 2000
    1,440 passengers, 63,000 tons
    PSR 43.7

11. MS (Unknown), October 2000
    1,380 passengers, 61,000 tons
    PSR 44.2   (Rotterdam Class)

ROYAL CARIBBEAN INTERNATIONAL

"Like No Vacation on Earth." The name of the cruise line was changed in 1997 from Royal Caribbean Cruise Line (RCCL) to Royal Caribbean International (RCI). Royal Caribbean was formed during January 1969 and originally was a partnership. During the 1980s, RCI began building large ships with modern designs. In January 1988, RCI launched the Sovereign of the Seas, the largest cruise ship at that time. The company attached royalty names, such as Sovereign, Monarch and Majesty, to its first three mega-ships. This was followed by names of allusions of uplifting and glorious feelings in the Vision-Class ships which began with the Legend of the Seas.

The current RCI project series is Vantage-Class and Eagle-Class ships (see ships at end of RCI text). The Voyager of the Seas, at 142,000 tons, boasts a twelve million dollar art collection, contains an ice skating rink, rock climbing wall, four decks of cabins with atrium street views plus other entertainment options. The ship is 1,020 feet long and 157.5 feet wide and is the first ship of RCI that does not transit the Panama Canal. Royal Caribbean has large ships and is building larger ones. Some of their ships are as tall as the Statue of Liberty's head and longer than three football fields. Beginning with RCI's ship, Legend of the Seas, and the "Vision" series ships, cabins are larger. Cabins of the older ships are small. Most cruises are medium priced with some priced slightly lower. In mid 1997, RCI bought and merged with Celebrity Cruises under the name of Royal Caribbean Cruises, Ltd. Celebrity maintains its own identity.

THE WORLD OF ROYAL CARIBBEAN

RCI ships visit Alaska, the Bahamas, Bermuda, Canada, the Caribbean, Europe, the Far East, Hawaii, Mexico, New England, the Panama Canal, the Mediterranean, and

Scandinavia. RCI's global sailings consist of sixty-four itineraries with one hundred and twenty-six destinations.

PASSENGERS

Royal Caribbean generally carries a good spread of passenger ages. The age of passengers approximates 70% under 50 years of age and 30% over 50. There may be a slightly older age group on longer cruises, depending on itinerary and time of year. There are a lot of shipboard activities for all ages. If you like less lines and a more quiet cruise, then you may want to select a small ship.

The lifestyle is more casual than formal and there are a great deal of passenger participation activities. Typically, RCI is a good cruise line for the first time cruiser and family. It has both casual and semiformal ships (newer ships). RCI lifestyle tends to be more casual than Celebrity, Princess and Holland America Cruise Lines. RCI allows repeat customers discounts when purchasing items in their on board shops. Royal Caribbean has a large number of repeat passengers.

SHIPS

Royal Caribbean International has approximately fifteen ships. This number varies from year to year.

1. MS Sovereign of the Seas, January 1988/96, 2,276 passengers, 73,192 tons, PSR 32.1

2. MS Nordic Empress, June 1990 1,606 passengers, 48,563 tons, PSR 30.2

3. MS Monarch of the Seas, November 1991, 2,354 passengers, 73,941 tons, PSR 31.4

4. MS Majesty of the Seas, April 1992 2,354 passengers, 73,941 tons, PSR 31.4

5. MS Legend of the Seas, May 1995 1,804 passengers, 69,130 tons, PSR 38.3   (Project Vision Class)

6. MS Splendour of the Seas, March 1996 1,804 passengers, 69,130 tons, PSR 38.3   (Project Vision Class)

7. MS Grandeur of the Seas, November 1996, 1,950 passengers, 74,140 tons, PSR 38.0   (Project Vision Class)

8. MS Rhapsody of the Seas, April 1997 2,000 passengers, 78,491 tons, PSR 39.2   (Project Vision Class)

9. MS Enchantment of the Seas, June 1997, 1,950 passengers, 74,140 tons, PSR 38.0   (Project Vision Class)

10. MS Vision of the Seas, April 1998 2,000 passengers, 78,491 tons, PSR 39.2   (Project Vision Class)

11. MS Voyager of the Seas, November 1999, 3,114 passengers, 142,000 tons PSR 45.6 (Project Eagle I)

12. MS Explorer of the Seas, September 2000, 3,114 passengers, 142,000 tons PSR 45.6 (Project Eagle II)

13. MS Radiance of the Seas, February 2001, 2,000 passengers, 85,000 tons PSR 42.5 (Project Vantage I)

14. MS Adventure of the Seas, April 2002 3,114 passengers, 142,000 tons PSR 45.6 (Project Eagle III)

15. MS Brilliance of the Seas, June 2002, 2,000 passengers, 85,000 tons PSR 42.5 (Project Vantage II)

CELEBRITY CRUISES

"Exceeding Expectations." Celebrity Cruise Line was formed in 1989 from Chandris Group which was Greek based and founded years earlier. Celebrity Cruises has a modern sophistication and is slightly more contemporary than Holland America. Their gourmet dining, decor and service are excellent. They provide activities for everyone. The Century, Galaxy and Mercury have a special smoking room which has a very intimate setting. It has been named after one of the owners and is called "Michael's Club." Excellent hand made cigars are available for purchase and can be smoked along with your favorite beverage in this elegant room.

Celebrity is similar to Holland America with its level of entertainment. They take great pride in their fine cuisine as well as providing excellent dining room service. The cruise line prices its cruises slightly above the medium price level, but is an excellent value for the money spent.

The Millennium class is a progression from Celebrity's Century-class vessels, which have been very successful. There are two new ships scheduled for delivery. One in June 2000 and another during January 2001 with a possible two more ships later. The cruise line has a four and five star fleet.

THE WORLD OF CELEBRITY

Celebrity has thirty-two itineraries with fifty-one destinations. Ports are in Alaska, the Bahamas, Bermuda, Canada, the Caribbean, Europe, Mexico, New England and the Panama Canal.

PASSENGERS

Most of the passengers are young couples, singles, a large middle age group with a nice share of seniors, depending on dates of sailing. Approximately 50% appear to be below the age of 50 and 50% above the age of 50. Celebrity provides nice daily attractions and fine shows for all ages. Greek influence is sometimes stiff. The cruise line is good for people who appreciate fine food and service. Celebrity is a good value for the money.

SHIPS

Celebrity has approximately six ships. This number varies from year to year.

1. MV Horizon, May 1990
   1,354 passengers, 46,811 tons,
   PSR 34.5

2. MV Zenith, April 1992
   1,374 passengers, 47,255 tons,
   PSR 34.3

3. MV Century, December 1995
   1,750 passengers, 70,606 tons,
   PSR 40.3

4. MV Galaxy, November 1996
   1,870 passengers, 77,713 tons,
   PSR 41.5

5. MV Mercury, November 1997
   1,870 passengers, 77,713 tons,
   PSR 41.5

6. MV (Unnamed) June 2000
   1,950 passengers, 85,000
   PSR 43.5   (Millennium I)

7. MV (Unnamed) January 2001
   1,950 passengers, 85,000
   PSR 43.5   (Millennium II)

8. MV (Unnamed) May 2002
    1,950 passengers, 85,000
    PSR 43.5   (Millennium III)

PRINCESS CRUISES

"It's The Love Boat." The cruise line was formed originally in 1836 as the "Peninsular Steam Navigation Company," a British Company. Later, in 1965, the company was founded with one ship, the "Princess Patricia." From this ship the "Princess" company name emerged. Princess Cruises found a beginning in 1965. The Peninsular and Oriental Steam Navigation Company (P&O), London, the parent company, formed Princess Cruises, as we know it in 1974. In 1988 Princess picked up Sitmar (an Italian line) thus the Italian influence. Princess is based in the Los Angeles area. The Island Princess and the Pacific Princess were the two ships used in the old television series "The Love Boat". Although early on, the Sea Princess was also used. The Sun Princess has been used in the follow-on television show, "The Next Wave." Princess' "Grand Class" fleet expansion program began with the introduction of Sun Princess in late 1995. When all ordered ships are delivered, Princess will have 13 or 14 ships.

Princess gives a very nice cruise with excellent service, food and quality entertainment. The cruise line has very fine ships and service oriented crew members. Many of their ships offer 24-hour dining. Princess places considerable emphasis on quality of food. They seldom repeat a dish during a cruise. The cruises are priced slightly above a medium level.

According to passenger surveys, Princess ranks with Royal Caribbean International, Celebrity and Holland America in high passenger satisfaction with many repeat passengers. Princess was selected by the U.S. Coast Guard for the prestigious award recognizing excellence in marine environmental protection. This was the first time a cruise line has received such an award.

THE WORLD OF PRINCESS

Princess offers over 70 itineraries ranging from seven to 64 days, sailing to six continents. Princess sails to Alaska, Panama Canal, Hawaii, the Caribbean, Tahiti, South Pacific, Costa Rica, Mexico, Europe, Africa, Holy Land, Canada/New England, South America, Asia and India. Princess combines cruising with inland attractions.

PASSENGERS

About 55 to 60% of the passengers are above the age of 50 and 45 to 40% are below the age of 50. Princess ships are excellent for first time cruisers and have an attractive following of repeat customers. Passengers tend to dress slightly above the medium level of semiformal cruising (such as Holland America and Celebrity). Princess actually has ships and not "boats" as portrayed in the "Love Boat" television series. However, the theme is still played on board. Passengers can get married or renew their wedding vows aboard some of their ships.

SHIPS

Princess Cruises has approximately twelve ships. This number varies from year to year.

1. MV Pacific Princess, May 1971, April 1975, September 1992,
640 Passengers, 20,636 tons,
PSR 32.2

2. TSS Sky Princess, May 1984, May 1992, 1,200 passengers, 46,000 tons,
PSR 38.3

3. MV Royal Princess, November 1984
1,200 passengers, 45,000 tons,
PSR 37.5

4. MV Crown Princess, July 1990
1,590 passengers, 70,000 tons,
PSR 44.0

5. MV Regal Princess, August 1991
1,596 passengers, 70,000 tons,
PSR 43.8

6. MV Sun Princess, December 1995
1,950 passengers, 77,000 tons,
PSR 39.4

7. MV Dawn Princess, May 1997
1,950 passengers, 77,000 tons,
PSR 39.4

8. MV Grand Princess, May 1998
2,600 passengers, 108,806 tons,
PSR 41.8

9. MV Sea Princess, December 1998
1,950 passengers, 77,000 tons,
PSR 39.4

10. MV Ocean Princess, February 2000
1,950 passengers, 77,000 tons,
PSR 39.4

11. MV (Unnamed), April 2001
2,600 passengers, 109,000 tons,
PSR 41.9

12. MV (Unnamed), October 2001
2,600 passengers, 109,000 tons,
PSR 41.9

DISNEY CRUISE LINE

"Discover Uncharted Magic." Disney's first ship, the Disney Magic, began sailing July 30, 1998. A ship designed to provide areas and activities for children, adults and families. The magic adventure is for kids from age three to twelve. Disney provides 15,000 square feet of deck space dedicated just to children. Teens can also enjoy a place created especially for them. Disney has very nice entertainment and quality productions. There is no casino on the Magic or Wonder.

The Port Canaveral Terminal, Florida, was built specifically for Disney Cruise Line. The facility features a one-of-a-kind 13,000 square foot terrazzo tile floor map of the Caribbean and the Disney sailing routes. It also contains models of the Disney ships.

THE WORLD OF DISNEY

A Disney Cruise Line vacation combines three, four or seven days of magical adventures at Walt Disney World Resort with a three or four day Bahamas cruise round-trip from Port Carnival, Florida. Cruises call at the historic Port of Nassau and spend a day at Disney's own private pleasure island, Castaway Cay, in the Bahamas where there is a 500 foot dock. The sister ship, Disney Wonder launched in 1999.

PASSENGERS

Passengers will normally be young to middle age couples, late 20s to late 40s, with small to teenage children. There are also singles and grandparents. Ages will vary according to time of year. Expect 70% to 75% under age of 50 and 25% to 30% over the age of 50. Young to middle-aged parents and older grand parents accompany their children. If Disney theme parks excite you, probably a Disney cruise will also.

SHIPS

Disney has two ships.

1. Disney Magic, July 1998, 1,750 passengers, 83,000 tons, PSR 47.4

2. Disney Wonder, June 1999, 1,750 passengers, 83,000 tons, PSR 47.4

NORWEGIAN CRUISE LINE

"Theme Cruises and Sports Programs." Norwegian Cruise Line was formed in the 1960s with a ship named the Norway, built in 1962. The Norway is a large ship with a 34.5 feet draft that will more often than not need tenders for passengers at some ports. The Norway, formerly the SS France, like the QE2, has distinctive features of the grand old ocean liners. Its latest, extensive refurbishment was completed in 1993. The cruise line places considerable emphasis on certain themes, fitness and sports and is therefore good for family cruises. Their ships are divided for smokers and non-smokers. The port side cabins of the ship are for non-smokers. Norwegian Cruise Line has good medium priced cruises and has fine entertainment, food and service. The cruise line purchased Orient Cruise Lines and the Marco Polo during 1998.

SELECTING A CRUISE LINE AND SHIP

THE WORLD OF NORWEGIAN

Norwegian Cruise Line has ships that sail to New England/Canada, Alaska, Hawaii, Mexico, Panama Canal, the Caribbean, Bermuda, South America, Europe, Mediterranean, New Zealand and Australia. Norwegian also sails from the Port of Houston, "Texaribbean" itineraries.

PASSENGERS

Some of the Norwegian lifestyle covers most ages rather well and is good for the first-time cruiser. Normally there is a good split of younger and older passengers and in some cases the younger generations may be larger, 55% under 50. Children to teens programs are very good as are the sports and special interest programs. There may be a slight edge to older adults (above age 50) on the Norway depending on the theme, length of cruise and time of year.

SHIPS

Norwegian Cruise Line has approximately eight ships. This number varies from year to year.

1. SS Norway, February 1962, June 1980, September 1993, 2,032 passengers, 76,049 tons, PSR 37.4

2. MS Norwegian Sea, June 1988
1,504 passengers, 42,000 tons,
PSR 27.9

3. MS Norwegian Dream, December 1992
1,750 passengers, 46,000 tons,
PSR 26.2

4. MS Norwegian Wind, May 1993
1,750 passengers, 46,000 tons,
PSR 26.2

5. MS Norwegian Crown, June 1988,
March 1996, 1,050 passengers, 34,250
tons, PSR 32.6

6. MS Norwegian Star, November 1973/
1991/1995 May 1997, 800
passengers, 28,078 tons, PSR 35.0

7. MS Norwegian Majesty, September
1992/1997/March 1999, 1,460
passengers, 38,000 tons, PSR 26.0

8. MS Norwegian Sky, August 1999
2,400 passengers, 78,000 tons,
PSR 32.5

COSTA CRUISES

"Cruising Italian Style." Costa Cruises is the largest cruise line in Europe. It is headquartered in Miami, Florida; an Italian company with a modern fleet of ships, worldwide itineraries and a distinct Italian personality. During June of 1997, Costa Crociere was purchased by Carnival Corporation and Airtours plc., but has continued to operate independently.

SELECTING A CRUISE LINE AND SHIP

Costa's history can be traced back to 1860, when Giacomo Costa began an olive oil business in Genoa, Italy. After his death in 1916, his three sons inherited the business and later purchased the 1,100 ton freighter Ravenna in 1924 to transport olive oil. By 1942, Costa had nine freighters. Costa's passenger service began in 1948 and in the late 1950s Costa launched its first new liner. Costa celebrated its 50th year of cruising in 1998.

With the boom in cruising during the late 1980s, Costa streamlined its fleet and expanded its area of operation. The flagship Costa Victoria has elegant Italian marble, Italian mirrors, murals, fabrics, glass and carpeting. Older ships are let go and new ships are added. You can take on Italy's favorite pastimes such as pizza dough tossing, Italian Karaoke, Bocce Ball and Tarantella dancing. You will experience Italian hospitality, authentic Italian cuisine and Italian-inspired theme nights. Caribbean cruises sail from Ft. Lauderdale, Florida starting at reasonable prices.

THE WORLD OF COSTA

As Europe's number one cruise line, Costa's fleet of Italian flavor (but multi-national crew) spans the globe, visiting sixty-three countries including the Caribbean, the Mediterranean, Northern Europe, South America and the Far

East. Transatlantic cruises are offered in both spring and fall.

PASSENGERS

Costa's age spread is fairly even with approximately 50% over the age of 50 and 50% under the age of 50. Costa is a good cruise line for someone who wants to cruise in a more European (Italian) atmosphere. Overseas, there will normally be announcements in several different languages. Most likely there will be more varied nationalities other than Americans or Canadians, depending generally on itinerary.

SHIPS

Costa Cruises currently has an international family of seven ships. This number varies from year to year.

1. MV Costa Riviera, November 1963/May 1995
   974 passengers, 31,500 tons, PSR 32.3

2. MV Costa Marina, 1969/July 1990, 770 passengers, 25,000 tons, PSR 32.4

3. MV Costa Classica, January 1992,
   1,300 passengers, 54,000 tons, PSR 41.5

4. MV Costa Allegra, December 1992
   800 passengers, 30,000 tons, PSR 37.5

5. MV Costa Romantica, November 1993
   1,350 passengers, 54,000 tons, PSR 40.0

6. MV Costa Victoria, July 1996, 1,950 passengers, 76,000 tons, PSR 38.9

7. MV Costa Atlantica, May 2000, 2,112 passengers, 84,000 tons, PSR 39.7

CARNIVAL CRUISE LINES

"The Most Popular Cruise Line In The World." Carnival also likes to be known as the "The Fun Ships." Carnival was formed in 1972 with one ship, the Mardi Gras, formerly the Empress of Canada. In 1975, the company purchased the Empress of Britain which entered service as the Carnivale. That was followed by the S.A. Vaal, which after a refurbishment, entered service in 1978 as the Festivale. That same year, Carnival announced the construction of a new cruise ship, the Tropicale, which joined the fleet in 1982. Three new cruise ships followed, the Holiday in 1985, the Jubilee in 1986 and the Celebration in 1987. They propelled Carnival to its current position as the largest cruise line in the world.

The cruise line purchased Holland America Line and Windstar Cruises in 1989. Carnival Cruise Lines, Inc., went public in 1987 and is traded on the New York Stock Exchange. The parent company was renamed Carnival Corporation in 1994 to better distinguish between it and the Carnival Cruise Lines operating brand. It is the parent company of Carnival Cruise Lines, Seabourn Cruise Line,

Costa Cruise Line, Cunard Line, Ltd., Holland America Line and Windstar Cruises, plus other business ventures. Carnival tends to build large ships with newer ones even larger. The lifestyle, colors, sounds and light combinations of many Carnival ships may jar your senses, but Carnival is successful at what it does.

Carnival initiated the first non-smoking ship, with it's Paradise, the last ship of their Fantasy Class. Passengers must sign a form prior to embarkation stating they understand the smoke free environment policy. Severe penalties are imposed on violators of the smoking ban. Do not smoke on the Paradise!

THE WORLD OF CARNIVAL

Carnival operates sailings ranging from three to 16 days to such areas as Alaska, Hawaii, Panama Canal, Mexican Riviera, West Coast, Canadian Maritime Provinces, the Caribbean and Bahamas. Cruises start from Miami, Port Canaveral and Tampa, FL; New Orleans, LA; Los Angeles, CA and San Juan, Puerto Rico.

PASSENGERS

Carnival ships are generally glitzy and most carry a very contemporary theme and lifestyle similar to theme parks. Much of this is enjoyed by children, teens, singles and young adults. There are 70% younger adults and children 20 - 30% older adults, over age 50, fewer seniors than on the more upscale cruise lines. Carnival seems to be a favorite with young honeymooners looking for an affordable getaway. Carnival's rates are generally lower than the other cruise lines in the same medium category. They have a wide variety of dining, activity and entertainment options. For an average cruise line, they do it well.

Carnival carries a very broad spectrum of people from many different backgrounds and is very casual. It is extremely important to be familiar with a specific ship of the fleet and its lifestyle before you plan to book a cruise on one. Some past passengers of Carnival who were interviewed say Carnival's price is right for the quality of cruise you experience.

SHIPS

The Carnival Cruise Line has approximately eighteen ships. This number varies from year to year.

   1.   MS Tropicale, January 1982/89/94
         1,022 passengers, 36,674 tons,
         PSR 35.8

   2.   MS Holiday, July 1985/94
         1,452 passengers, 46,052 tons,
         PSR 31.7

3. MS Jubilee, July 1986
1,486 passengers, 47,262 tons,
PSR 31.8

4. MS Celebration, March 1987
1,486 passengers, 47,262 tons,
PSR 31.8

5. MS Fantasy, March 1990
2,044 passengers, 70,367 tons,
PSR 34.4

6. MS Ecstasy, June 1991
2,040 passengers, 70,367 tons,
PSR 34.4

7. MS Sensation, November 1993
2,040 passengers, 70,367 tons,
PSR 34.4

8. MS Fascination, July 1994
2,040 passengers, 70,367 tons,
PSR 34.4

9. MS Imagination, July 1995
2,040 passengers, 70,367 tons,
PSR 34.4

10. MS Inspiration, March 1996
2,040 passengers, 70,367 tons,
PSR 34.4

11. MS Carnival Destiny, September 1996
2,642 passengers, 101,353 tons,
PSR 38.3

12. MS Elation, February 1998
2,040 passengers, 70,367 tons,
PSR 34.4

13. MS Paradise, November 1998
2,040 passengers, 70,367 tons,
PSR 34.4

14. MS Carnival Triumph, July 1999
    2,758 passengers, 102,000 tons,
    PSR 36.9

15. MS Carnival Victory, Fall 2000
    2,758 passengers, 102,000 tons,
    PSR 36.9

16. MS (Unnamed), Fall 2001
    2,100 passengers, 82,000 tons,
    PSR 39.0

17. MS Carnival Conquest, Fall 2002
    2,758 passengers, 102,000 tons,
    PSR 36.9

18. MS Carnival Glory, July 2003
    2,758 passengers, 102,000 tons,
    PSR 36.9

ORIENT LINES

"The Destination Cruise Specialists." Orient's 800 passenger flagship Marco Polo has received high ratings in exciting destinations and itineraries by national travel magazines. It has done well in other ratings also. Orient does not seem to have an on board party, high-energy atmosphere, the Marco Polo exudes more of a cultural holiday experience. Orient is excellent for the adventurous. We recommend children be teenagers before sailing on the Marco Polo. Orient offers gracious service and is a good cruise value.

The line offers detailed port lectures and on-board cultural performances to enhance the destination experience. Distinguished guest speakers are sometimes on-board. On longer cruises, a larger percent of passengers will be over the age of 50. The Marco Polo is capable of sailing long distances without re-provisioning food, fuel and fresh water. The ship is stable, even in 10 to 12 feet waves. Orient is owned by Norwegian Cruise Line.

THE WORLD OF ORIENT

Orient Lines specializes in exotic destinations offering port-intensive cruise vacations to Australia, New Zealand, the Mediterranean, Italy, Turkey, the Black Sea, Spain, French Riviera, Portugal, Malta, Africa, Indian Ocean, Asia, Greek Isles, Egypt and even Antarctica. Many of their cruises feature pre-cruise and post-cruise packages. Early bookings receive a discount.

PASSENGERS

Depending upon the itinerary, it may be well to have sailed on a cruise or two before cruising with Orient --unless you are adventurous. Those who would like a small ship with diverse destinations and longer times in port would enjoy Orient. Passenger ages may vary with the seasonal itineraries, but a good spread of ages above and below the age of 50 can be expected with above 50 having the edge.

Orient offers moderately priced seven to 27 day cruise-tour vacations to six continents. The Marco Polo is a midsize ship.

SHIP

    1.   Marco Polo, April 1965/1991/October 1993
           800 passengers, 22,080 tons, PSR 27.6

AMERICAN HAWAII CRUISES

"The Way Hawaii Was Meant To Be Seen." The American Hawaii Cruises is a sister line to The Delta Queen Steamboat Company. In 1993 American Hawaii Cruises was acquired by The Delta Queen Steamboat Company; the headquarters consolidated in New Orleans, Louisiana during 1997. The American Classic Voyages Company, Inc., is the parent company of both The Delta Queen Steamboat Company and the American Hawaii Cruises. American Hawaii Cruises plans major expansion that will double the company's fleet. They are building two new, privately funded cruise ships, which are being constructed in U.S. shipyards on the Gulf coast. Something that hasn't happened in more than forty years. American Classic Voyages is awarding contracts for two 71,000 ton ships to eventually replace the Independence, which is nearly fifty years old.

THE WORLD OF AMERICAN HAWAII

There are many wonderful things to experience in Hawaii. It's impossible to fit them all in during a fly-to visit in the course of a week or so. Passengers can discover the beauty and individuality of Oahu, Kauai, Maui and the Big Island of Hawaii during seven leisurely cruise days. There is so much history available including the World War II bombing of Pearl Harbor and surrounding facilities.

The only difficult decision that cruisers must make is deciding how to spend their free time in ports. Passengers can sight see by car, submarine, catamaran, Zodiac raft, kayak, helicopter, biplane, parasail, horseback, bicycle, motor coach, or on foot. The islands offer beautiful golf courses. Hawaii is a paradise!

Numerous cruises throughout the year feature special themes such as Whales in the Wild, Big Band, Aloha Festivals and Hawaiian Heritage. The cruise line carries Hawaiian ambience in its decor. Part of the ship's program includes Hawaiian history, legends, royalty, gods and goddesses. Passengers can participate in the study of ancient and modern hula, chants and language.

PASSENGERS

There is a good spread of age and family fun. Normally there will be 50% below the age of 50 and 50% above the age of 50. Cruises range from three, four or seven nights. Expect passengers to be dressed as they would on any one of the Hawaiian Islands.

SHIP

The line has one ship with more being planned.

1. S.S. Independence February 1951/June 1980/1994/1997, 809 passengers, 30,090 tons, PSR 37.1

OVERVIEW OF LUXURY SHIPS

For the most part, the more expensive cruise lines sail smaller ships and fewer passengers with perhaps a higher crew to passenger ratio. They may have slightly larger and perhaps more lavish staterooms. There is some extra performance with food and service when comparing a four star dining room with a five star plus or six star. The top, more panache cruise lines will normally provide higher levels of food, service and ambience. Courtesy and service are exacting, but accomplished in a manner that puts passengers at ease. Dress during the day is elegantly casual. Gentlemen may be encouraged to wear a suit or coat and possibly a tie for dinner several nights during the cruise with some formal attire required for both ladies and gentlemen.

The luxury cruise lines offer a certain elegance and spaciousness. They provide high quality furnishings, crystal glasses, bone china, utmost care, attention, hospitality and exude gracious living. You can say the luxuries have "style with substance." Discuss with your travel agent the cruise value of one or more of these more expensive, but excellent, cruise lines.

LUXURY CRUISE LINES

Here is a listing of the more formal, luxury and highly rated cruise lines. These cruise and tall ships are very nice with some being "the epitome of cruise sophistication." Many of these ships become more formal in dress and activities, except for the water sport and adventurous Windstar tall ships. A discussion of each cruise line follows.

Crystal Cruises
Cunard Line, Ltd.
Radisson Seven Seas Cruises
Seabourn Cruise Line
Silversea Cruises
Windstar Cruises (boarder on a sport luxury)

(Note: The following four pages contain ship photos.)

MS Carnival Destiny
Carnival Cruise Lines

MS Mercury
Celebrity Cruises

MS Enchantment of the Seas
Royal Caribbean International

MS Galaxy
Celebrity Cruises

SS Independence
American Hawaii Cruises

TSMV Queen Elizabeth 2 (QE2)
Cunard

MS Norwegian Wind
Norwegian Cruise Line

MS Veendam
(Photo courtesty Holland America Line)

MS Sun Princess
Princess Cruises

MV Costa Victoria
Costa Cruises

MS VistaFjord (MS Caronia)
Cunard

MV Crystal Symphony
Crystal Cruises

CRYSTAL CRUISES

"Five-Star-Plus Service." In 1988 Crystal Cruises was incorporated in Los Angeles, California. A design team was set up and a contract was signed for the building of Crystal Harmony at Mitsubishi Heavy Industries in Nagasaki, Japan. In June 1990, Crystal Harmony was delivered and in July christened by Mary Tyler Moore. The Crystal Harmony's maiden voyage was out of San Francisco to Alaska.

In April 1995 Crystal Cruises celebrated delivery of Crystal Symphony. The Symphony was built in Turku, Finland. She was christened by Angela Lansbury in New York Harbor. The Symphony's maiden voyage was from New York City to Los Angeles. Crystal Cruises, with these two luxury cruise ships, set out to redefine luxury cruising throughout the world. Crystal Cruises is owned by Nippon Yusen Kaisha (NYK), one of the largest shipping companies in the world.

Crystal's European-trained shipboard staff strive to maintain the highest service standards possible and have earned numerous top awards. Entertainment aboard the ships provide a well balanced variety, including seminar series featuring well-known artists and enrichment speakers, historians, humorists, Broadway production shows and classics. The casino is the first Caesar's Palace at Sea.

Crystal ship's interiors are dignified, but are not especially eye catching architecture. Most luxury comes from their attention to detail and doing the extras to pamper and satisfy passengers. With a variety of cuisines and specialty restaurants, guests can dine each evening and never repeat a menu. The dining room personnel will do almost anything to please a dinner guest. It seems nothing is too difficult. Exceptional food and service are provided all the time. Employees are happy to be part of Crystal.

THE WORLD OF CRYSTAL

Crystal ships cruise nearly all over the world. Australia, New Zealand, South Pacific, the Orient, Western Europe, Baltic Sea, the Mediterranean, Black Sea, Red Sean, Greece, Italy, Turkey, France, South America, the Caribbean, Panama Canal, Alaska, Canada, Mexico and Hawaii. Crystal also offers land programs.

PASSENGERS

Crystal Cruises provide impeccable service which is enjoyed by many repeat and seasoned cruisers. The Cruise line is rated very high by top travel magazines. Age groups are 65% over the age of 50 with 35% under 50. If you care for personalized attention, top service and sophisticated ambience, you will like Crystal.

SHIPS

Currently, Crystal has two ships.

1. MV Crystal Harmony, July 1990, 940 passengers, 49,400 tons, PSR 52.5
2. MV Crystal Symphony, April 1995, 940 passengers, 51,044 tons, PSR 54.3

CUNARD LINE, LTD.

"Getting There Is Half The Fun." Cunard is an old line that dates back to the year 1840 when the first paddle-wheel steamer Britannia crossed the Atlantic in 11 days. Cunard has had British, Norwegian and American flavor. Cunard was a pioneer in the early Atlantic crossings of ocean-going liners. Carnival Corporation owns the "lion's share" of Cunard. As mentioned earlier, Carnival merged Cunard with Seabourn so there are some ships that changed names. Cunard/Seabourn's vessels range from very small, luxury ships to large ships, most notably the QE2 whose character or national rating extends through three classes from standard to luxury. Mauretania Class tends to be a cross between standard and premium, Caronia Class is premium and Grill Class is considered luxury. The QE2 has five separate dining rooms for the various class passengers. Such an arrangement presents some drawbacks.

MV Seabourn I (Sea Goddess I) and MV Seabourn II (Sea Goddess II) are small ships carrying only 116 passengers. With the crew number coming close to matching passengers, service indulges everyone's whim. The two ships rank high in luxury and ambience. Nearly all amenity expenses are included at time of booking. Cruisers on these two ships are usually affluent. Activities and entertainment are minimal.

THE WORLD OF CUNARD

Cunard has a variety of cruise routes and destinations. The transatlantic has always been a favorite route for Cunard's QE2 which is still one of the fastest ocean liners. Ships cruise the Caribbean, transatlantic, Europe, Adriatic, British Isles, Orient, South America, Panama Canal, New England/Canada, Bermuda, Africa as well as other areas of the world.

PASSENGERS

Certain ships of Cunard seem to have an older crowd and seasoned cruisers. The smaller luxury ships of Cunard draw more passengers over the age of 50 and are mostly couples. However, the QE2 draws people from all ages and walks of life depending on the time of year and destinations. The reason for this is people are attracted by publicity of this famous ship. The QE2 has had it's ups and downs. Some passengers love the ship while others were not impressed. Dress on Cunard is casual during the day and occasional semiformal to formal during dining.

The four ships listed after QE2 on the following list are more apt to display more total luxury class than the QE2. Except, perhaps, the MS Caronia (Vistafjord) which depending on your outlook, could be considered a cross between high premium and luxury class. (Cunard Line) Cunard/Seabourn has approximately five ships.

SHIPS

1. TSMV Queen Elizabeth 2, May 1969/1987/94/96, 1,715 passengers, 70,327 tons, PSR 41.0

2. MS Caronia (Vistafjord), May 1973/84/94/97, 732 passengers, 24,492 tons, PSR 33.4

3. MV Seabourn (Sea Goddess I), April 1984/95/97, 116 passengers, 4,260 tons, PSR 36.7

4. MV Seabourn (Sea Goddess II), May 1985/95, 116 passengers, 4,260 tons, PSR 36.7

5. MV Seabourn Sun, (Royal Viking Sun) December 1988/1993/96, 740 passengers, 37,900 tons, PSR 51.2

RADISSON SEVEN SEAS CRUISES

"Upscale Luxurious Adventure." Radisson Diamond Cruises and Seven Seas Cruise Line merged operations in 1995. Radisson Hotels International expanded into this luxury realm of travel. Like Seabourn, Radisson Seven Seas prefers small ships which provide a cruise with personalized, elegant and posh service. On board activities are limited. Passengers generally consist of senior executives and professionals. The twin-hulled SSC Radisson Diamond has a revolutionary design, which makes it a stable ship that sails at fairly slow speeds of up to 12 knots. It is difficult to get seasick on this ship. We would not recommend this ship for first time cruisers.

THE WORLD OF RADISSON

Radisson Seven Seas has a variety of worldwide itineraries. This includes the Mediterranean, Northern Europe, Scandinavia, Arctic, Greenland, Iceland, Asia, South America, Panama Canal, the Caribbean, Galapagos, Tahiti, Bora Bora, Moorea plus other interesting ports of call.

PASSENGERS

Radisson Seven Seas ships carry less than 500 passengers. Many passengers are frequent cruisers who enjoy small ships. This helps insure personal service. There are not many on board organized activities, and entertainment is limited. Ships are roomy and have excellent passenger flow. Dress is casual during the day, but semiformal to formal during evening dining. Most passengers are over the age of 50.

SHIPS

Radisson Seven Seas has approximately seven ships.

1. MS Song of Flower, 1986/February 1990, 200 passengers, 8,282 tons, PSR 41.4

2. MS Bremen, November 1990/ November 1993
164 passengers, 6,752 tons, PSR 41.1

3. SSC Radisson Diamond, May 1992, 354 passengers, 20,295 tons, PSR 57.3

4. MS Hanseatic, March 1993, 184 passengers, 8,378 tons, PSR 45.5

5. MS Paul Gauguin, January 1998, 320 passengers, 19,125 tons, PSR 59.7

6. MS Seven Seas Navigator, August 1999, 490 passengers, 30,000 tons, PSR 61.2

7. MS Seven Seas Mariner, February 2001, 720 passengers, 46,000 tons, PSR 63.8

SEABOURN CRUISE LINE

"For The Discriminating." Seabourn was formed in 1987 by a Norwegian industrialist. The idea was to sail ships carrying small numbers of passengers and provide them with priority service and style. There are limited activities. Most who sail with Seabourn are affluent from the U.S. and Canada. Others are wealthy Europeans. Evening dress is normally semi-formal to formal in a fancy and posh environment. Seabourn says it defines the art of luxury travel. The Carnival Corporation, by a consortium, owns a large portion of Seabourn and after completing acquisition of the Cunard Line, Carnival Corporation merged Cunard with Seabourn. In May of 1998, Seabourn Cruise Line and Cunard Line became one new luxury cruise vacation company under the banner Cunard Line Limited. Both will continue to operate as separate lines.

THE WORLD OF SEABOURN

Seabourn sails on worldwide itineraries. Cruise lengths normally vary. Many cruises range from ten to fourteen days, others extend well over twenty days. Seabourn itineraries can take you to Canada, Alaska, the Caribbean, Panama Canal, Australia, South Pacific, South America,

Asia, the Mediterranean, Europe, Scandinavia, British Isles, the Baltic plus other areas that may be planned.

PASSENGERS

Seabourn passengers are generally experienced cruisers with high expectations and usually affluent professional people. Some passengers can be 40 to 50 year old business owners and professionals, yet others may be older. Usually there are many repeat cruisers on Seabourn. There are limited activities and entertainment, but excellent service and dining. An average age breakdown would be 65 to 70% above the age of 50.

SHIPS

Seabourn has approximately three ships.

1. MS Seabourn Pride, December 1988, 204 passengers, 10,000 tons, PSR 49.0
2. MS Seabourn Spirit, November 1989, 204 passengers, 10,000 tons, PSR 49.0
3. MS Seabourn Legend, March 1992/July 1996, 204 passengers, 10,000 tons, PSR 49.0

SILVERSEA CRUISES

"The Tangibles of Luxury Travel." In the early 1990s, the Lefebvre family of Rome, former owners of Sitmar Cruises, conceived and organized a unique cruise company to build and operate luxury cruise ships. The name "Silversea" was chosen because the founders felt it connotes quality and luxury as well as capturing the romance and special sensations of the sea. Silversea began promoting cruises in 1993 for its inaugural cruise in April 1994. Silversea Cruises Ltd. is headquartered out of Ft. Lauderdale, Florida.

Silversea has an open, single seating dining room, an elaborate show lounge, an Italian crew and European staff. They have an all inclusive price featuring: all suite accommodations, round-trip economy air transportation, deluxe pre-cruise hotel stay, all gratuities, all beverages, including select wines and spirits, all port charges, all transfers and porterage.

Silversea has been quite successful winning numerous prestigious awards. It has garnered the highest possible accolades from leading travel magazines and guide books. The ships are rated among the best cruise ships of the world.

THE WORLD OF SILVERSEA

Worldwide itineraries and destinations include Africa, Madagascar, the Seychelles, the Far East, China and

Vietnam, the Indian Ocean and Red Sea, Australia, New Zealand, Northern Europe, Canada/New England, the Caribbean, the South Pacific, the Mediterranean, the Baltic and South America.

PASSENGERS

Silversea passengers are usually well travelled and well cruised. Passenger lists consist mostly of couples, but occasionally there may be singles. You will find more affluent passengers over the age of 50; mostly American with some British, Canadians and few Europeans. Children are on board infrequently. There is single, open seating dining featuring luxurious elegance. If you are interested in special attention to detail, this line could be for you. Silversea ships have a crew to passenger ratio of nearly one-to-one. Entertainment and activities are less than on larger ships. After your first sailing you will become members of "Silversea's Venetian Society" and are offered savings on future cruises.

SHIPS

Silversea has approximately four ships. Silversea holds an option for two additional ships in the years 2002 and 2003.

    1.   MV Silver Cloud, April 1994,
            296 passengers, 16,800 tons, PSR 56.7

2. MV Silver Wind, January 1995,
296 passengers, 16,800 tons, PSR 56.7

3. MV (Unknown), July 2000,
396 passengers, 25,000 tons, PSR 63.1

4. MV (Unknown), May 2001,
396 passengers, 25,000 tons, PSR 63.1

WINDSTAR CRUISES, "THE TALL SHIPS"

"180 Degrees From Ordinary." Holland America also owns Windstar Cruises, which is another type of cruising that offers superb sailing and cruising at its best. It is laid back and has a casual, but a very nice atmosphere. These are four or five mast, tall sail ships. Sails are mainly automated for operation and at the press of a button sometimes the ships cruise under sail as well as power. They cruise at speeds approximately one half of a large cruise ship. They frequent many ports and isolated beaches that other power cruisers do not. Pricing is slightly above the average.

Although Windstar does not quite meet all luxury standards, they are up-scale sailing/power ships with a yacht-like lifestyle. Windstar is placed in this section, but could be listed as premium. Leading travel magazines have rated the ships rather high for an all-around, elite sportsman's cruise. For those who enjoy on board and off board water sports, and do not care for the formality of a large cruise ship, Windstar will fit the bill very nicely.

THE WORLD OF WINDSTAR

There are four computer-directed luxury, small sailing ships: Wind Star, Wind Song, Wind Spirit and Wind Surf which sail in the Mediterranean, the Caribbean, Costa Rica and perhaps elsewhere as the desire hits.

PASSENGERS

The passengers are usually young to middle age couples, singles and include a nice age spread. A good mainstream for singles to meet. Passengers are mainly American at an average age of 48 years with many between the ages of 35 and 50. Some seniors and few children. Dress is casual during the day and "elegantly casual" for evening dining. A sport coat during dinner is optional and usually at your discretion. There can be approximately one-third Windstar repeaters. If you are physically challenged, you should check with your travel agent first to determine what is available for ease of sailing. Expect less entertainment and on board activities than on a large cruise ship. Water sports abound and you can enjoy the warm tropical breezes.

TALL SHIPS

Windstar has approximately four tall sailing/power ships.

1. MYS Wind Star, December 1986
   148 passengers, 5,350 tons, PSR 36.1

2. MYS Wind Song, July 1987
   148 passengers, 5,350 tons, PSR 36.1

3. MYS Wind Spirit, April 1988
   148 passengers, 5,350 tons, PSR 36.1

4. MYS Wind Surf, February 1990/98
   312 passengers, 14,745 tons, PSR 47.2

DELTA QUEEN STEAMBOAT COMPANY RIVER CRUISES

"Steamboatin' Theme River Cruises." A type of cruise that does not seem to receive as much publicity, but is becoming more and more popular is the "Steamboatin' River Cruises." These can be booked on America's inland waterways through Mark Twain's America.

The Delta Queen, which is designated as a National Historic Landmark, entered service in 1927. She is propelled by a paddlewheel powered by steam. An expression came from steamboats that we still use today. That is "letting off steam." When pressure in the boilers became too high, valves had to be opened to release the pressure. Thus, we release our pressure by "letting off steam."

The Delta Queen Steamboat Company, which was originally the Greene Line Steamers, was founded in 1890. The company now has three steamboats (and yes, they can be called "boats"). The Legendary Delta Queen, the Mississippi Queen and the American Queen. The Mississippi Queen began cruising the rivers in 1976 and the American Queen made her debut in 1995.

The Delta Queen is 285 feet long, has four passenger decks, carries 174 passengers and a crew of 75. The Mississippi Queen is 382 feet long, has seven decks, transports 414 passengers and a crew of 156. The American Queen, 418 feet long, has six passenger decks and carries a normal load of 436 passengers and a crew of 180. The company has plans for approximately five new additions to its fleet.

THE WORLD OF THE DELTA QUEEN COMPANY

Based in New Orleans, Delta Queen Steamboat Company offers three to fourteen night river cruise vacations throughout the heartland of America.

There are currently four regions these classic steamboats cruise:

> The American South Region: New Orleans to the Mississippi River and Arkansas River's junction and New Orleans to Galveston, Texas on the Intracoastal Waterway.

Crossroads of America Region: Arkansas River delta to Tulsa and to St. Louis on the Mississippi River.

America's Heartland Region: St. Louis to Minneapolis/St. Paul on the Mississippi River and to Ottawa on the Illinois River.

Wilderness Rivers Region: Ohio, Kanawha, Tennessee and Cumberland Rivers.

Departure cities include:

New Orleans	Little Rock
Memphis	Nashville
Cincinnati	Pittsburgh
St. Louis	Chattanooga
Minneapolis/St. Paul	Galveston
Louisville	Ottawa

These cruises are excellent for "down home America." The passengers are mainly middle aged. Not so many children or younger adults, although good history and geography lessons are available. The price of a cruise is above the average price for cruise ships, but most people interviewed say the cruise is well worth it. The interior of the boats is typically Victorian. The American Queen is the largest, it and the Mississippi Queen offer more amenities.

Guest stars/celebrities offer entertainment on board. This can be Jazz, Dixieland, other themes and good old southern hospitality. The theme cruises are popular. We recommend you go 'steamboatin' on one of these fine ladies during the spring, early summer or fall. A midsummer cruise could be hot in the southern region. The south is beautiful in the early spring with all the foliage. If you are a Civil War buff or historian, this cruise would excite you.

PASSENGERS

If you are interested in American History, heritage and nostalgia with a closeness to land and enjoy a very relaxed pace, you would enjoy the "Steamboatin' River Cruises." There is usually a good mix of ages especially on short trips; but the above 50 age group out-numbers the below 50 on longer river trips, 65 to 70% versus 35 to 30%. There isn't much for young children to enjoy. Dress is casual during the day and elegantly casual some evenings. Some dinners will be semiformal with coat and tie. Emphasis is on American regional cuisine.

BOATS

The Delta Queen Steamboat Company has approximately three boats.

1. Steamboat Delta Queen, 1927/1998 174 passengers, 3,360 tons, PSR less than 20.

2. Steamboat Mississippi Queen, 1976/1996, 414 passengers, 3,364 tons, PSR less than 20.

3. Steamboat American Queen, June 1995, 436 passengers, 3,707 tons, PSR less than 20.

RIVER CRUISES

Europe, Egypt and China as well as other countries offer river cruises also. Among these are the Danube and Eastern Europe, Amsterdam and Holland's Waterways, Canals of Burgundy, Great Rivers of Europe, the Rhine River Valleys, Russian Waterways and Finland, Ancient Egypt and the Nile River and China and the Yangtze River. These cruises can vary from one day to sixteen days.

BARGE "CRUISING"

"Leisurely Pace." Barge "cruising" is popular in Europe. Barges "cruise" the canals and inland waterways of Europe during the warmer months of mid April to late October. They move along at a slow pace during the day and as evening approaches, stop near a village for sight seeing and usually stay docked for a smooth nights sleep. The barges normally "cruise" for three to fourteen days transiting German, French, Dutch, English and Irish rivers.

These countries offer considerable scenic beauty for passengers on board. Sometimes meal specialties are prepared from local ports and villages. Entertainment is very limited. Depending on the barge, this totally casual "cruise" can accommodate ten to twenty four passengers. Check with your agent whether to take children.

The United States also has a certain amount of flair for river barge "cruising" on the Mississippi, Ohio, Cumberland and Missouri rivers.

FREIGHTER AND CARGO SHIPS

"A Slow Boat To China." To sail on a freighter or cargo ship takes a lot of patience, time and the ability to do without all the activities and luxuries of a cruise ship. If you have the time and do not care where you go, when you get there or how long you will stay, then a freighter or cargo ship would be a good adventure for you. It is like "taking a slow boat to China." Some freighters and cargo ships have stopped transporting passengers because of the problems involved with passenger needs and comfort. However, freighter cruises are a bargain and are good for the adventurous.

The cabins have good accommodations and are normally larger than many cruise ship cabins. The meals are good with a casual atmosphere. A few freighters may have a semiformal night occasionally but normally not a formal night. Whether a doctor or a medically trained person is on board depends on the company and the number of crew members and passengers. Freighters usually do not have the wing-like stabilizers for controlling roll that are common to a cruise ship. With over 12 passengers there normally will be a doctor or medically trained person on board. It would be best to check first. Children should be teenagers to go on a freighter. Also, seniors do go, but should be in good health to attempt the cruise. There is a senior age limit on most freighters which could range from 72 to 82 and after a specified age a doctor's certificate may be required. Check to see whether the ship can handle the physically challenged. Freighters normally are not equipped to handle wheelchairs.

Ports of call can change periodically and in some instances as soon as the cargo is unloaded or loaded, the ship could depart the port. Other times they may stay several days. Usually there are certain major ports that a freighter is scheduled to frequent. Their mission is to pick-up and deliver freight and cargo as expeditiously as possible. This could mean they may be diverted at times. Freighters normally will dock at cargo areas away from the main passenger terminals. Tours and excursions may be taken at many of the ports of call. Be sure to take along a guidebook for the areas you will visit.

The freighters spend many days at sea. If you want to read books or even write a book, perhaps a freighter cruise would fit the bill. There is little entertainment, but usually the price is right. Reading material, a VCR and videos will normally be available. The cost could run from $50.00 a day to over $200.00 a day. Tipping is either optional or somewhat similar to cruise ship suggestions. Passenger numbers could vary from just a few to 50 or even nearly as high as 100. No pets are allowed.

Ports to contact for freighter cruises lie on the east coast such as the New York and New Jersey areas. Also there are locations all along the west coast and the gulf coast at locations such as Houston, Gulfport and New Orleans. Overseas ports can also be contacted for freighter cruise information. Your travel agent will have the means to contact them for you.

Freighter travel is not for everyone. Take a freighter to relax with few people to see parts of the world that you may not see on a cruise liner. And, depending on your nature, freighters may be a fine mode of travel to get away from it all, sail to far parts of the world and into the sunset...

CHAPTER SIX

TRANSPORTATION AND HOTELS

CRUISE LINE AIR/SEA TOTAL PACKAGES

Cruise lines offer total vacation packages. They will make airline reservations, set up transportation and baggage handling and arrange for hotels when necessary. Some passengers prefer this choice. It is convenient and saves time and effort. There are advantages and disadvantages in using this process. Sometimes these total packages are priced right and are "good deals" and sometimes not. When looking up hotel prices in cruise brochures be aware that the prices listed may be for each person and not per room. Check with your travel agent for a comparison in cost between cruise line flight prices and what you pay separately for your flight.

Cruise lines sometimes can receive a break on prices for hotel accommodations. Normally, there is a set price for flying costs as published in brochures and quoted through your travel agent. Since costs of flying fluctuates due to supply, demand and seasons, it could be less costly to pay for your own flight. You can select your schedule and fly on the airline you desire. If the cruise line schedules your flight you will be compelled to fly the airline and the schedule they select. Sometimes, for a fee, a cruise line may let you alter the schedule or airline slightly. Seniors who use the senior discount books/coupons or passengers with frequent flier miles can book a less expensive flight.

Most airlines and many regional carriers offer booklets or coupons for senior fares. The age for this is 62. Consider this option as it will save you money. Coupons or booklets are usually valid for one year from the issue date and are normally good for United States travel only (including Hawaii, Puerto Rico, Alaska and some parts of Canada). The following are some of the major airlines that have this option: America West, American, Continental, Delta, TWA, United and US Airways. Check a particular airline you have servicing your area to see whether they sell books or coupons for seniors.

If you choose the air/sea package offered by the cruise line, and the flight is delayed on the day of sailing due to labor problems, weather or aircraft maintenance, you must notify the cruise line headquarters on the "800" phone number provided. They will advise you on what course to take. Cruise line officials have the option of delaying sail away. If you schedule your own flight and it is delayed beyond sailing time, the ship will not wait for you. If you book your own transportation to the port, you should plan to arrive at the city of embarkation at least one day early if the flight arrival time is close to the ship's departure time. If for any reason your flight is delayed and the ship leaves as scheduled, it is up to you, at your expense, to catch the ship at the next port.

Luggage is another issue when you have the cruise line schedule your flight. You will be met at the airport by cruise line representatives (usually in uniform and/or holding up a sign) and taken by bus or minivan to the ship or hotel. In some cases you may claim your luggage and then turn it over to the cruise line personnel for their transfer to the ship. Usually, the cruise line personnel will pickup your luggage after your flight and transfer it to the ship. You may not have seen your luggage since you departed your home town airport. This could be an uncomfortable feeling. Make sure the luggage identity tags sent to you prior to your departure from home are securely fastened to your luggage handles so they are not torn off during handling.

SCHEDULING TRANSPORTATION AND HOTELS

If you schedule your own flight and arrive during the time the cruise representative is at the airport, you may have the option to use their baggage handling and transportation services. However, there will be a charge. This varies from $10.00 to $20.00 per person. The other alternative would be a limousine, taxi or bus. Depending on distance and traffic, many taxi fares may range from only $10.00 to $30.00 total, so this is certainly a consideration.

If you will be in the area for more than one day it could be worthwhile to rent a car. The major car rental agencies will usually pick you up and deliver you to the ship's dock by a rental car bus. Check this out before you rent. When special rates are in effect, or with discount coupons, it would be handy and more economical to rent a car than to pay a cruise line or taxi for several trips in transportation. Hertz and Avis are leaders with this type of service. Of course, turn in your rental car before you cruise. Courtesy transportation from hotels normally will not take you to the dock to catch your ship or pick you up after a cruise. They are usually confined to provide transportation from the hotel to the airport and vice versa.

Some cruises to the Caribbean and Panama Canal depart from San Juan, Puerto Rico. Occasionally the airline connections from the Continental United States (CONUS) is such that you may arrive in San Juan in the late afternoon. If this is the case you should make a decision whether to leave a day early and stay overnight in San Juan. Many hotels in San Juan are expensive so it pays to shop around. There are some hotels and bed and breakfast inns that are reasonable. The cruise line, using group rates sometimes can book a

TRANSPORTATION AND HOTELS

hotel room in certain resort areas for a little less money than you would pay without a corporate, AARP, AAA, or senior rate. Check the flying schedule carefully so you will arrive in time to catch your cruise ship. Be cautious about planning to arrive late in the day on the same day of your cruise. If the transportation system "hick-ups" you may be temporarily stranded.

Ships normally return after a cruise in the morning around 7:00 or 8:00 AM. It is best to have scheduled the time for your return flight near or slightly after 12:00 noon. This gives you enough time to disembark the ship and take care of the various responsibilities. The ship has to clear immigration, customs, agriculture and off-load luggage, plus other technicalities prior to the time the passengers disembark. You will need enough time to disembark, turn in your customs form, locate your luggage, board transportation to the airport and complete airport check-in. All non-U.S. citizens must report early on board ship the last morning to clear customs and immigration..

There are times when several cruise ships will arrive at a given port nearly the same time causing some congestion and possible delays. During your cruise, a travel form may be placed in your stateroom asking you to fill in your airline, flight number, day and time of departure. This will be done in order to get the early departures off the ship first. It takes time to disembark 1,000 to 2,500 people from a ship.

Cruise lines will normally offer tours upon returning to your port city for disembarkation. It is possible for the cruise line to take you to the airport after the tour as well as handling your luggage while you are on the tour. If you have a late afternoon flight departure, you can sign up for one of these tours. If the time of the tour is in the morning, the tour office on board the ship will have you meet in a certain area on the ship so that you can disembark in time for your tour. This is also true when you have an early tour at other ports of call during the cruise.

After you have cruised several times, you may consider taking a back-to-back cruise. One example is to select a seven day cruise on a particular cruise line that sails from Saturday to Saturday and after completing this cruise, remain overnight in a hotel at that port city. The cruise line will normally pick up the tab for your night at the hotel. Then you sail on another ship of the same cruise line to different destinations on Sunday for seven more days. You actually get two cruises for the price of one airfare.

Another example is to schedule two cruises on different cruise lines. Take a seven day cruise and disembark during early morning and embark on a different ship in the afternoon at the same port. This allows you the opportunity to enjoy two different cruise lines and two different ships. It is an exciting adventure! This works well when you have paid your own airfare. Back-to-back cruises are cost effective for people who travel from the west coast to the east coast, from Canada or overseas to distant ports. Be sure to arrange this with your travel agent before hand.

HOTEL SAFETY TIPS

When traveling anywhere and staying in a hotel, there are certain actions you need to take for your safety and the safety of your family. Here is a list of some actions to consider to help insure that safety:

>   Do not draw attention to yourself by displaying large amounts of cash or expensive jewelry.

>   Do not needlessly display guest room keys in public or carelessly leave them on restaurant or bar tables, at the swimming pool or where they can be easily stolen.

>   Be street-smart on the type clothing you wear. When returning to your hotel late in the evening, use the main entrance. Be observant and look around before entering parking areas.

Do not answer the door in the hotel room without verifying who it is. If a person claims to be an employee, call the front desk and check.

Do not invite strangers to your room.
Close the door securely whenever you are in your room and use all locking devices.

Do not leave valuables in your room. Check them at the desk's safe deposit box or take them with you.

Locate the exact location of fire exits when you first check-in.

If you see any suspicious activity, report your observations to the hotel management.

Ladies should be cautious about wearing clothing which is too brief attracting adverse attention. This also applies to any ports of call.

CHAPTER SEVEN

PACKING TIPS

PACKING

A major mistake cruise passengers make is packing every item they *think they will need.* You do not need all those items, you need the *right items.* The right clothing is the type and weight for the geographical location of your cruise. Pre-plan your wardrobe for each day and night of the cruise. Do not pack items you think you may need "just in case."

A good motto is: "When in doubt, leave it out."

Pack as you would for any resort destination with a touch of formal and semiformal dress. You may leave from a northern state in the cold of winter for a cruise in the Caribbean where temperatures are in the 80s. When leaving a cold climate, get by with wearing a light jacket so once you arrive at the point of embarkation it will not be too bulky to store.

There is no need to bring a trunk or several bulky suitcases. These are hard to deal with when traveling. Soft canvas or material suitcases with wheels usually work well. Some cruise lines recommend hard case luggage. For a seven day cruise, one large or medium suitcase per person and a small carry-on will suffice. Cruise lines prefer you not bring more than two suitcases per person, plus the carry-on. The smaller carry-on bag will be needed the last night of your cruise (see Chapter Twelve). And really, you do not need more than one large or two medium suitcases per person plus a smaller carry-on, unless perhaps, you are going on an extended cruise. On a large ship, the crew must handle over 4,000 pieces of luggage which takes time to deliver to each cabin. An important point, most cabins do not have a whole lot of closet and drawer space.

About three days before you depart home for your cruise, take out your suitcases and lay them on the floor of your bedroom. Start to pack odds and ends and some clothing that will not wrinkle easily. If everything is packed too early you will forget what you packed. It helps (particularly for ladies) if you make a list of combinations of clothing and accessories you plan to wear each day of the trip, and especially for evening wear. Some days you will need to change clothes two or more times.

The day before you leave, fold in the rest of your clothing as flat as possible and leave the suitcase open until the morning you leave in case you have left something out. Consider leaving some shirts, slacks, blouses, pants and dressy items on small, light, thin hangers. When you arrive aboard ship you can quickly hang them as is. Your cabin closet may be short of hangers and space. The day before you leave, close your suitcase(s) and lift them to see how heavy they are. Also, place a card with your name, address and phone number *inside* your luggage. Remember you will also need some space for the goodies you acquire on the trip. If your luggage is going to be a burden because of weight or bulkiness, you better reconsider what you have packed.

Taking carry-on bags only may not enable you to take all the required clothing and articles needed on a cruise. The main purpose of carry-on bags is for speed and mobility, and perhaps knowing you will have your bag at the destination. If you have to pack more than one large carry-on (within limits allowed on board aircraft) this could defeat your purpose. Consider carry-on bags for three or four day cruises. They are not recommended for seven day or longer cruises.

During the day aboard ship, dress casual with good taste. Cotton pants, shorts, loose shirts, sandals or sneakers will do fine. For an Alaska cruise the dress is layered to be warm or cool with shirts or blouses, sweaters, coats, rain slicker and pants. Normally, during the summer months in

Alaska, you will not need a large, heavy, bulky coat. When you go ashore, you need a comfortable pair of walking shoes. Wear a long sleeve shirt or blouse, sweater and windbreaker. Do not forget ultra violet protected sun glasses, a fold-up umbrella, sun block/sun tan lotion and a hat. They are all very important.

As pointed out in Chapter One, each and every cruise ship creates an atmosphere and presents a lifestyle and personality that is peculiar to the cruise line and the ship. Each ship is different. Some cruise lines have a more casual environment whereby passengers dress more casually for the functions aboard ship while other cruise lines require a more formal dress. Check the cruise brochure and/or discuss the dress with your travel agent. If you select a more formal cruise ship then you must abide by their dress codes.

Evenings are a special time on cruise ships. Cruise lines have two formal and a few semiformal evenings on seven day cruises and a proportionate more on longer cruises. If men enjoy dressing-up and looking "spiffy" with a dark suit, tuxedo, dinner jacket or sport coat and tie, and ladies with cocktail and party dresses, then the semiformal to formal cruise lines would be more for you.

Take along a plug-in night light, especially if you have children. The cabin light switches sometimes can be a problem to locate and lights tend to illuminate the whole cabin. A plug-in night light is very helpful for inside cabins. It is included on your packing checklist.

DRESS FOR LADIES

For tropical areas, take short sleeve tops and one long sleeve cotton or light weight cover up for air conditioned areas. Colorful tops will give flavor to your neutral shorts, pants and slacks. For your cruise wardrobe, we suggest that you select neutral colors such as navy, white, gray, brown, black and tan. These colors will void the need for several colors in accessories. No need to take several extra purses, belts, dress shoes, and so forth, to color coordinate. Include deck shoes such as sneakers, comfortable walking shoes and heels/pumps for dress. Ships have excellent exercise facilities so consider taking sneakers and a light workout outfit.

Strive to be comfortable. Be sporty and not shabby or sloppy. Dress to be confident. Around the swimming pool wear a comfortable bathing suit. It is wise to take two bathing suits. Be sure to take a non see-through cover-up, sandals or slip on shoes to wear with your bathing suit when you go from the pool to the buffet or your stateroom. Bathing suits should not be worn in public areas without cover-ups. Use jeans or denims sparingly. They are okay for tours off ship, or if the ship has a western night they can be worn. One pair of jeans is sufficient. Tennis shoes, jeans or shorts are not normally allowed in the dining room for evening dinner. Be aware of country customs so you do not offend by a too casual attire off ship.

For formal nights, pack an evening gown, cocktail, party dress or pants suit. It is nice to dress a little bit glamorous on informal nights too. Take a pantsuit and nice dress. Casual nights can be a blouse or shirt, skirt, slacks or pants and dresses are always attractive (again, no shorts, T shirts, tennis shoes or jeans). Dress elegantly casual.

For wear during the day on a seven day cruise, pack only two or three pair of shorts and two pair of pants. One pair of pants could be white or a light color. By mixing five to seven short sleeve shirts or blouses, you will look different each day. No need to take a different pair of shorts or slacks for every day. If you really want to pack light, plan on wearing an outfit early in the cruise and then again late in the cruise, alternating. For a seven day cruise, it is advisable to take combinations of three or four sets of changes. However, this would be the minimum because there may be times when you will wear two sets of clothes in one day. If there are laundry facilities on board the ship, this combination would work. Cruise brochures and travel agents will advise if laundry facilities are available.

Try to choose silver or gold and pearls for jewelry. Be wise in your choice. It is not necessary to drag along most of your jewelry. If your clothes have gold trim such as a buckle, take gold jewelry. If your clothes have silver trim take silver. If you have a little of both, take just a little of each to match. Some newer ships have hair dryers in cabin bathrooms. Most ships have 110 volts and 220 volts, but some foreign ships may have only 220 volts. These are items to checkout with your travel agent.

It is a nice experience and an honor to be invited to the Captain's table for dinner. Normally, guests selected to sit at the table are prearranged from the cruise line's main office or with the Captain and Maitre 'd deciding. Occasionally guests are invited at random. Being polite and a good conversationalist seems to help. Selection is sometimes considered from loyal repeats, VIPs, passengers occupying suites, and honeymooners. It is possible to politely ask the Maitre 'd or social hostess for a seat at the Captain's table for a given night. The competition is high so do not feel bad if you are turned down. Occasionally a highly valued travel agent to the cruise line can put in a good word for you. The Captain's guests must wear a dark suit and tie, tux or dinner jacket and the ladies a nice evening or cocktail dress when the Captain is present. He most likely will not sit at his table every evening due to his commitments. Sometimes other senior officers will have a table where guests may be invited.

DRESS FOR GENTLEMEN

On a seven day cruise take a dark suit and sport coat with two dress shirts and two or three different ties. If you do much cruising, it would be advisable to purchase a tuxedo or dinner jacket. The formal nights are great and the more you fully participate, the more fun they are. A tux can be rented aboard ship, but if you cruise fairly often it is less costly to buy a tux or dinner jacket. Some tux rental places sell tuxedos and dinner jackets at reasonable prices. Of course, a tux or dinner jacket can be used for other special functions. After you purchase a tux, you will have to be careful not to "outgrow" it.

Decide whether you want to wear shorts and slacks/pants in tans/browns or blues/grays. Then you can decide on shoes and accessories. Take a pair of sneakers and comfortable walking shoes. One or two bathing suits are a must. If you have nautical shirts and white pants, take them. On a seven day cruise, take five or six short sleeve shirts, two pair of casual shorts and two or three T shirts for around the pool.

For cruises to Alaska expect day temperatures during the summer months to be similar to the weather in the Great Lakes region. Far north daylight hours in mid to late June range from 17 to 19 hours. May and June are usually the driest months in Alaska. Late June through August can be short sleeve weather months. Plan on casual, comfortable clothing that you can easily shed or layer. Take along a wind breaker, sweater, medium-weight pants and a hat. Bring a fold-up umbrella. In May, temperatures will start to be in the 50s. You will not need a heavy, bulky coat during June through mid August when temperatures are in the low 60s and occasionally in the 70s and sometimes even reach the high 70s. During early September the weather will start to cool off to occasional 40s and 50s, and perhaps sometimes down to the mid 30s in the evening.

For longer cruises such as ten, eleven or twelve days, you need to add very little more to your seven day wardrobe. There may be one or two more formal nights and one or two more informal nights. The rest will be casual nights. Keep in mind overseas cruises will require modifications:

PACKING FOR DINNER DRESS

The following guide shows an example of what ships normally plan for casual, semiformal and formal evenings.

(EXAMPLE)

Cruise Length	Elegantly Casual	Semi-Formal	Formal
2 - 4 days	2 or 3	0 - 1	1
5 - 7 days	2 or 3	1 or 2	2
8 - 11 days	4 to 6	2 to 4	2 or 3
12 - 14 days	5 to 7	3 to 5	3 or 4
15 - 18 days	7 to 9	5 or 6	4 or 5
19 - 21 days	8 to 10	6 or 7	5 to 6

The preceding is an example of what ships normally have during a cruise from three to twenty-one days. Casual, semi-formal and formal times vary from one ship to another. Ships vary considerably on the number of semiformal and casual nights. Always check with your travel agent.

SUGGESTED PACKING CHECKLIST

Listed below is a suggested checklist for packing for a casual, semiformal to a formal cruise with one to three formal nights.

SEVEN DAY LIST FOR LADIES, GENTLEMEN AND FAMILY

General Items:

___ Cruise tickets (package)
   ___ Passports (or birth certificate and driver's license; passport is recommended)
   ___ Luggage tags
   ___ Travel information
___ Flight tickets
___ Consider a hang-up bag, *only if needed*,
___ One medium or small carry-on bag for the last night's cruise (See Chapter Twelve)
___ One large suit case per person (especially if handling your own flights and luggage)
___ Binoculars
___ Camera and camrecorder (if desired)
   ___ Four rolls of film (minimum)
   ___ Batteries (as required)
___ Suntan/sunscreen lotion, SPF 15 minimum
   Include UV protected dark glasses
___ Note pad
___ Travel journal and address book for memory recording and later reference
___ Small flashlight/pen light

PACKING TIPS

___ Small plug-in night light (especially if you take children or have an inside cabin)
___ Small sewing kit
___ Small first aid kit
___ Sterile handy wipes or hand sanitizer liquid
___ Travel books & maps
___ Travel alarm
___ Eye glasses
___ Telescoping Umbrella (Alaska cruise and other such climates)
___ Jewelry
___ Photo copies of front page of passports, driver's license and credit card(s) (Kept in separate location from originals)
___ Money, 1 or 2 credit cards (leave extra credit cards at home) Make copies of the first two pages of your passport and your credit card (store separately).
___ Dollar bills: Take several one dollar bills for tips enroute. Also, a couple of 5 dollar bills plus change
___ Post card stamps. (Local country stamps may be purchased at the Purser's desk.)

SEVEN DAY LIST FOR GENTLEMEN

___ Bill hat
___ Straw-type brim hat (if needed for added sun protection)
___ 3 sport shirts button (various colors, elegantly casual)
___ 2 or 3 sport shirts pull-overs that could include 2 T shirts
___ 2 pairs of casual shorts
___ 2 pairs of slacks color coordinate
___ 2 casual pants (one white or light color)
___ 2 or 3 regular ties to wear with a sport coat or dark suit
___ Belts as required
___ 2 dress shirts (1 short sleeve) If no tuxedo, then 3 dress shirts.
___ 1 sport coat
___ 1 dark suit or tuxedo and/or dinner jacket
___ Under shorts and shirts

___ 7 - 8 pair every day socks
___ 3 pair dress socks
___ 1 pair white shoes (if desired)
___ 1 pair sneakers/walking shoes
___ 1 pair beach shoes, thongs/sandals/slip-ons
___ 1 or 2 swimming suits and cover-up shirt
___ 1 work-out pants or shorts and T shirt
___ Wind breaker/jacket/rain slicker, sweater (Alaska and northern areas)
___ Light sweater or long sleeve warm shirt for air conditioned areas that may be cold
___ Handkerchiefs
___ Pajamas
___ Medication (keep in original bottle)
___ Shaving kit and toilet articles
___ Tuxedo
___ 1 pair tux shoes or dress shoes
___ 1 set suspenders
___ 1 or 2 tux shirts
___ 1 or 2 cummerbunds
___ 1 or 2 formal ties
___ 1 pair cuff links & studs

SEVEN DAY SUGGESTED LIST FOR LADIES

___ Two or three pairs of casual shorts
___ Two pairs long pants/slacks
___ Five to seven short sleeve shirts, T shirts, dressy blouses (mix)
___ One long sleeve shirt or blouse or sweater (for air conditioned areas)
___ One or two pair black heels/pumps for dress (or color as required)
___ One pair sneakers
___ One pair comfortable walking shoes
___ One or two pair of casual shoes
___ Two swim suits
___ One pair sandals/swim/beach shoes
___ Belts
___ Purses one or two for dress and one for daily use, (fanny pack is good)
___ Evening gown
___ Cocktail dress

PACKING TIPS

___ Party dress
___ Pantsuit
___ Colorful scarf or two
___ Night gown(s)
___ Under clothing
___ One or two skirts
___ Wind breaker/jacket/rain slicker (Alaska)
___ Sweater (Alaska)
___ Jewelry
___ Medicine (keep in original bottle)
___ Toilet articles
___ Money, 1 or 2 credit cards (leave extra credit cards at home) Make copies of the first two pages of your passport and your credit card (store separately).

For cruises over seven days, only add a few extras to cover the additional ports of call, days at sea and evening dress.

THINGS TO DO AT HOME BEFORE YOU LEAVE

1. Stop mail, newspapers, deliveries.
2. Set sprinklers (seasonal).
3. Phone calls (friends/relatives).
4 Plants and arrange for yard care.
5. Bills, letters.
6. Animal care (Note: Pets are not allowed aboard ships).
7. Someone to check on your home.
8. Electrical appliances needing attention.
    Consider unplugging certain electrical appliances. Especially in seasons and areas of electrical storms.
9. Advise family how to contact you in an

emergency (see back of cruise line brochure).

10. Check on your insurance coverage.

11. Appointments needing extension or cancelation.

12. Home security system and light settings. Light timers, if desired.

CHAPTER EIGHT

EMBARKATION AND LEARNING THE SHIP

PLANNING YOUR ARRIVAL

Plan to arrive at the ship's dock soon enough so you will have enough time to check in your luggage and have a few minutes to relax before you go aboard ship. For a tip, porters will be available to handle your luggage. While you are waiting to board is a good time to meet some of your fellow passengers. Later, on board the ship, you will find a different atmosphere from what you may have had leading up to embarkation. People will be more friendly, cordial and relaxed. You will find you have something in common with someone. A friendly smile will do wonders. A cruise ship is a great place to make new friends. Everyone is there for one purpose... to have fun and enjoy a great cruise!

On the day of embarkation, try not to eat a big breakfast or lunch because there will be a delicious 'welcome aboard buffet' available as soon as you board the ship. Ships usually sail in the afternoon or evening. This allows time in the morning for the passengers on the previous sailing to leave the ship and for the ship's crew to make ready for the new set of guests. As a rule, the new passengers can board the ship a few hours prior to the sail time. Check with your travel agent or the brochure for the time you may start boarding. In no event should you plan to board later than 30 minutes prior to advertised sailing time because at sailing time there will be an "All Aboard" and perhaps a "toot" from the ship's horn and the gangway will be raised!

BOARDING PROCEDURES

When first preparing to board the ship, orderly lines are formed for registration and for picking up your cruise card. A certain portion of the dock may be assigned to you as noted on your ticket to board the ship, so fully review your ticket. You must fill out your boarding forms PRIOR to arriving for embarkation. Sometimes the ship's terminal will have the registration desks assigned by the first letter of your last name or by cabin number. Normally, there will be a longer line for registration just prior, during and immediately after the time stated for boarding. If you desire a short line, a later boarding time of an hour or two will accommodate you.

Just as you are about to board the ship, a photographer will take your picture (if you desire) with a background of art work of the ship you will be sailing on. Take the time to have this picture taken and consider wearing something

EMBARKATION AND LEARNING THE SHIP

nautical for the boarding photo. This photo will appear in the ship's photo gallery later during the cruise and it may be purchased for approximately $6.00 if you desire. It will become a very nice reminder of your cruise. Savor every part of your embarkation and your cruise. The cruise time will go so very fast! Your attitude is important as to how you will enjoy the entire cruise. Become involved as much as you can. Meet and enjoy the people around you, it will pay dividends. Above all keep a smile and be patient!

The excitement increases the moment you step aboard the ship. As you board the ship you will be greeted by friendly crew members and directed to your stateroom. Survey your cabin to make sure everything is all right. There should be orange life vests in the closet or on the bed. Note the time of the practice lifeboat mustering drill which will include your life vests. This drill is a requirement just as the safety briefing is prior to takeoff with commercial aircraft, and it is a fun thing to do. But be cognizant of what you are to do, where and when, in the event of an emergency. There is also a certain seriousness about this drill. Refer to Chapter Ten for all the essentials.

Insure that the key or key card unlocks your door. Your dinner table assignment may be noted on the boarding card or a card within your packet of information. When you have a chance, review the ship's directory of services booklet in your cabin, it contains valuable information. Be sure to make use of the "Do Not Disturb" or "Make Up Room" cards. Review the daily bulletin for the day's activities. Carry this with you at all times. Some cruise lines print their bulletin in several different languages. Royal Caribbean prints their bulletin, the "Cruise Compass" in English, French, Spanish and German.

Check the way from your cabin to the nearest stairway and to the nearest emergency exit. Note where the fire alarm is located also. If a member of your party has a disability such as mobility, sight or hearing, notify the Cabin Steward so he/she will be aware of it and can offer aid in an emergency if needed.

Once you have oriented yourself to where your stateroom is located (note forward or aft, portside or starboard) then start exploring the ship. This is exciting! But remember there is a great welcome-aboard buffet being served topside. So work your way up to that area.

Your baggage should arrive at your stateroom an hour or two later, sometimes it may take a little longer. When you receive your luggage, unpack your items placing them in the drawers and closets. Place the empty suitcases under your bed. You may have to lift the bed slightly to push them under.

Ships are a "cashless society" except for the casino and a couple of other announced functions. The card you were issued when you arrived for embarkation serves as a charge card to purchase items aboard ship. It is used as identification to permit you to enter the ship at various ports of call so take special care of it and carry it with you at all times. If you desire, you can report to the designated desk upon your arrival on board and a Purser representative will make an imprint of your charge card. At the end of the cruise when you receive the glad tidings of your bill for on board charges, all you need to do is review it for accuracy. Otherwise, if you desire to pay in cash the last day of the cruise you must report to the Purser's desk to pay in person. Usually ships have a limit on amounts of money for check writing or some may not take personal checks. Travel agents will be aware of various cruise line's finance requirements.

VALUABLES

Nearly all the newer ships have safes in each cabin. The safe is either locked with your own code numbers or the magnetic band on your personal credit card. Be sure when you leave your cabin you lock your special value items in the safe. You are responsible for securing your valuables and although the cabin steward is trustworthy, it may be possible for other people to enter your cabin without the cabin steward knowing it. There are also secure provisions at the Purser's desk. Theft is not normally a problem on board ships.

LEARNING YOUR WAY AROUND THE SHIP

The first day and evening aboard is time to get to know the ship. Explore as much as possible so you will know where areas are located. Set yourself some landmarks (seamarks) on the ship so you can orient yourself. You will run into passengers who are wandering and wondering which way to go for certain functions. This could happen the entire seven days of a cruise unless you orient yourself with some way to help you find your way around the ship, especially on the larger ships.

Let's pause here for some trivia that may be of interest to some of you. How did we come-by "Port" and "Starboard?" A possible derivation of these two words goes back to the early days of sailing ships. There was a certain kind of vessel which had a "steering board" suspended over the side of the ship which acted as a rudder. The steering board was suspended over the right hand side of the vessel and so this side become known as the "steering board side" which was eventually abbreviated to starboard.

When these vessels came into the harbor it was safer to berth with the left hand side of the ship against the pier, thus avoiding damage to the steering. The left hand side of the ship became known as port side.

Time and time again, on the larger ships especially, passengers become disoriented and somewhere in the middle of the ship it is difficult to tell port and starboard and the bow from the stern or which way the ship is going. When passengers are attempting to locate a particular area, bar, dance floor or dining room they have difficulty with their bearings. There are several ways to have aids, cues and mental notes to assist in orienting oneself to the various locations.

The first way is to have points of reference when you are inside and cannot see the water to know which direction the ship is moving. Knowing where the bow or stern are will help considerably. Normally, a ship will locate the fitness center and things-to-do areas at one end of the ship. The dining rooms, some cocktail areas and certain bars may be located at the other end of the ship, normally aft. The casino is normally located near mid ship so the 'glitzy' and noise of it catches your eye and ear as you walk through. The largest show room is normally located in the bow of a ship.

Another way to orient yourself is to make special note of how the atrium is situated and which way the elevator or stair entrances are pointed (to stern or bow). Note which side of the ship the Purser's desk is on, again - starboard (right) or port (left). Make a mental note of certain areas that will point you either forward or aft. An example which works for many ships (but not all) is to look at the center hand railing on all of the stairways. Normally either the top (upper most end) or bottom (lower most end) will point to either stern or bow on all stairways. Pick one and remember it. Knowing the preceding cues is solving half of the problem. Knowing the direction the ship is sailing helps a whole lot. Of course when you have been on the ship for several days, direction will start to come naturally - but then it is time to disembark.

DEVISING A LOCATOR CARD

By referring to the brochures at home, it is possible to put together a small location card that can be carried with you throughout the ship. This lists key areas, the decks they are on and whether they are located forward, midship or aft. A helpful suggestion that takes some effort is shown below. Make it a game or challenge with whomever you are with to be able to locate areas effectively. Eventually, locating the areas will come naturally. The following is an example for Holland America's "MS Veendam:"

MS VEENDAM

*Deck numbers may be added after boarding.

EMBARKATION AND LEARNING THE SHIP

*12	Sports Deck	Fwd	Crow's Nest.
		Mid	Tennis Courts.
11	Lido Deck	Fwd	Observation, Juice Bar,
		Fwd	Ocean Spa, Gym,
		Fwd	Beauty Salon, Pool.
		Aft	Lido Restaurant, Terrace.
10	Navigation Deck	Fwd	Bridge, Cabins.
		Aft	Swimming Pool.
9	Verandah Deck	All	Cabins.
8	Upper Promenade	Fwd	Show Lounge Balcony,
		Fwd	Atrium, Terrace, Boutique,
		Fwd	Ocean Bar, Kiosk.
		Mid	Casino, Shop Arcade,
		Mid	Figurehead Gallery, Puzzle,
		Mid	Card Room, Explorers Lounge,
		Mid	Library.
		Aft	Upper Rotterdam Dining Room.
7	Promenade Deck	Fwd	Main Show Lounge, Dance
		Fwd	Floor, Photo Gallery, Purser,
		Fwd	Atrium, Shore Excursions Office.
		Mid	Wajang Theater, Hudson Room,
		Mid	Half Moon, Main Galley.
		Aft	Lower Rotterdam Dining Room.
6	Lower Promenade	Fwd	Cruise Director, Hotel
		Fwd	Manager Offices, Atrium, Cabins.
5	Main Deck	All	Cabins.
4	A Deck	Fwd	Doctor's Office.
		Mid	Cabins.
		Aft	Cabins.

You can go back and underline or highlight the areas most frequented so they will be easily identified. The ships will normally furnish a similar card that can be carried with you, but not as detailed as the above information.

After you have made your way to the "welcome-aboard buffet" and have started adding those extra calories, it is time to circulate around the ship and get ready for the "Sailing Away Fun." There will be great music and festivity, especially in the Caribbean, because everyone is excited and cannot resist a happy, congenial mood, so put on your happy face! You will want to be topside near the swimming pool when the ship sails away. Don't miss it!

If you are dining with the main seating and have an afternoon sail-away, you need to start thinking about getting ready for dinner. The first night at dinner is normally elegantly casual. But remember, no shorts, tennis shoes or shirts without collars. Jeans are not recommended at dinner. It is a tradition at sea to dress for dinner in a manner that is not sloppy or shabby. The waiters, assistant waiters, Maitre 'd and staff will be dressed formally. They take great pride in what they do. It would be an insult to your fellow passengers and to the dining staff to not dress elegantly casual. You will have plenty of time to go casual the next day. Most likely the next evening will be a formal evening as it will be the Captain's welcoming, reception cocktail party and dinner.

"KNOTS" AND A "LOG"

The ship's captain will be announcing the speed of the ship in "knots", as twenty nautical miles per hour. A knot is actually a measurement/unit of speed equal to one nautical mile per hour and is used for measuring the speed of airplanes, ships and boats. A nautical mile is equal to 1.15 land (statute) mile. A nautical mile is equal to one-sixtieth of a degree on the earth's surface and measures 6,080.2 feet. Near the equator, one minute of longitude is equal to one nautical mile. As you go north or south from the equator, the size of a degree gradually becomes smaller. Navigators, when measuring distance on their charts use an average location for distance along the ship or aircraft's course.

How about some more trivia? The word "knot" is derived from the ancient sailors practice of gradually trailing a line over the side of the ship that was knotted at specified intervals . The number of spaced knots fed out in a specific period of time was calculated for the ship's speed. To prevent the line from moving with the ship a large piece of wood, or log weighted at one end, was attached to the trailing end of the line to hold it in place on the surface of the sea . Hence, yet another definition is explained, the ship's "log." These days, the ship's log is a record of all the pertinent information regarding the sailing of the ship's position, speed, arrivals, departures and a host of other important data.

Okay, let's move on to dress, customs and etiquette...

CHAPTER NINE

SHIPBOARD DRESS AND DINING

DRESS, CUSTOMS AND ETIQUETTE

Although we live in a casual world, it will add considerable quality and enjoyment to your cruise to dress appropriately for prescribed evening dinners. It is actually fun to do so. This custom dates back to the time ships were primarily ocean liners. To follow the ship's request for dress at dinner typifies the ceremony of cruising. Dressing for dinner is a tradition that creates an excellent atmosphere and certainly adds value to your cruise. Chapter Seven contains packing tips that will help you prepare for your cruise.

The ship's daily activity bulletin, placed on your bed or table each evening by the cabin steward, will dictate the dress for dinner the next day and lay out the next day's schedule of events. *Be sure to read this carefully.* It helps to highlight the activities that interest you.

A personal note. Be considerate of your fellow passengers and the ship's crew. Dress according to what is suggested in the ship's bulletin for a certain evening. Continue to wear the dress stipulated, not only for dining, but throughout the evening.

Normally, dress will be casual the first and last nights of your cruise. As a rule, when the ship is in port, the dress is also casual. The Captain's welcome aboard cocktail and dinner party, early in the cruise, is a formal evening. Gentlemen are encouraged to wear a dark business suit and tie, a tuxedo or dinner jacket, while the ladies wear evening gowns/party cocktail dresses or pantsuits. The gentlemen look handsome and the ladies look glamorous! This creates an air about the ship that is seldom duplicated in our day-to-day lives because of our present day casualness. It is well worth it to fully participate in this formal atmosphere and it is a common courtesy expected during the entire evening. You have the option of changing clothes after dinner only when suggested by the theme of the ship's bulletin or Cruise Director. It is discourteous to other guests and staff to change into very casual dress after dinner on a semiformal or formal night.

During a seven day cruise there normally will be two formal nights for dinner. The longer cruises of 12 to 16 or so days may have three or four such nights depending on the schedule and cruise line's policies. Participate, participate! You will enjoy your cruise to the fullest. The other dinner

SHIPBOARD DRESS AND DINING

evenings will be semiformal or casual requiring dinner guests to follow the dress code; but above all, no T shirts, shorts, tennis shoes, denims or jeans during dinner! This is in keeping with the fine, five star dining provided by outstanding, dedicated waiters and dining room staff who display considerable pride and effort in their work. Those who serve you will be dressed fashionably. It would be an insult to them and to other passengers to come to dinner not dressed appropriately.

One of the areas often abused is the dress code aboard ship. The ship's crew is very reluctant to politely correct a passenger for not following the dress code. It is more up to the manners and respect of others to wear proper dress when requested. Sometimes passengers enforce the dress and courtesy themselves--which is acceptable. Informal or semiformal are sometimes used to describe the same type of dress. As a general guide:

Formal evenings: Ladies: A dressy outfit such as a long gown, pantsuit or party/cocktail dress.

	Gentlemen: A dark suit and tie, dinner jacket, or tuxedo. Prefer a suit over a sport jacket.
Semiformal evenings:	Ladies: An informal cocktail dress, pantsuit or (Informal) dressy skirt and blouse.
	Gentlemen: A suit or jacket/sport coat and tie, dress shirt and slacks.
Casual evenings:	Ladies: A pantsuit or sporty outfit, dress skirt and blouse or nice slacks (elegantly casual).
	Gentlemen: A sport shirt with collar and slacks (elegantly casual). No T shirts, jeans or tennis shoes, unless it is a theme night.

Cruise ships encourage passengers on formal and semiformal evenings, to continue to wear the requested dress of the evening not only to dinner but also throughout the evening. This creates an air about the ship that is classy. Anymore, in our day to day life, we have become extremely casual and dress mostly in jeans, tennis shoes, shorts and T shirts. But aboard ship, there is a certain elegance that dinner and evening brings that is seldom matched at home. Fully cooperate with it, you will certainly enjoy the evening much more.

On formal nights the chief steward, maitre d's, waiters and assistant waiters all dress in fine fashion. They display a great deal of pride in their appearance and service. The Captain and his staff, which include the Cruise Director and hostesses, all dress formally. The dinner tables are elegant with tablecloths, napkins, fine crystal and dinnerware. Go with the dress code, it will pay dividends, make you feel good about yourself fitting in for a really great evening.

Professional photographers will be taking pictures of the guests at various times. Individual and group portraits can be scheduled. The photos taken during the formal evenings will be cherished for years to come.

DINING

On many ships with two dinner seatings, you will be assigned an evening dining table. The ship's maitre d'hotel and his staff will make every effort to give you your choice of early or late dining. This assignment will be made based upon your request at the time you made your reservation and seating availability. On late bookings, your requested seating may not be available. Dining is one of the most important aspects of the cruise experience, therefore it is important that you are happy and enjoy your fellow table guests. Generally, by the end of the cruise you will have become good friends with your dinner mates. This relationship enhances your cruise enjoyment. However, for one reason or another, if you do not enjoy the company of those selected to dine with you, there is an option. Contact the ship's maitre d'hotel or the head waiter and ask to be moved to another table. They will gladly oblige your request if possible. This will be accomplished very discreetly. Be sure to make your request the first or second day of the cruise. The longer you wait, the more difficult it may become to change tables.

Evening dining times of most ships are enforced in order to accommodate dinner guests efficiently. On many ships the times must be strictly observed. In this event, the dining room staff may close the dining room doors a few minutes after serving has started. The polite thing to do is to be ready for dinner when it is to be served. Also, the first sitting must be out of the dining room at the appropriate time so that the second sitting my enter on time. On luxury ships with just one seating, passengers may enter the dining room at their leisure.

Most ships will accommodate low fat, salt-free, low-carbohydrate, vegetarian, Kosher or other diet preferences. This request must be made well in advance, preferably at booking. Advise your travel agent of this requirement. It would be wise to touch base with the maitre d'hotel or head waiter to confirm your request prior to sitting down for your first dinner.

By the second night of the cruise, during dinner, the waiter and assistant waiter will probably know your likes and dislikes and attempt to please your every wish. Your every need and desire may be anticipated before you know you wanted it.

Breakfast, lunch and dinner are provided on the upper decks and casual attire can be worn. Casual wear can also be worn in the dining room for breakfast and lunch, but no bathing suits. While in your swim suit, pizza, hamburgers, hot dogs and similar eats are generally available around the pools. A well planned, well laid out buffet is also available. Guests sometimes use this nice buffet for a quick breakfast or lunch.

When at the swimming pool during the day and passengers decide they would like to partake in the inside buffet or return to their stateroom, they are requested to put on a bathing cover-up over their swim suit and wear some form of sandal, slipper or shoe on their feet. Bathing suits should not be worn in the buffet area or public rooms without a cover-up. Nor is it appropriate to walk barefooted. There are several reasons for this, two important ones are health standards and consideration for other passengers. Being polite aboard ship is extremely important and gratifying.

DINING ROOM ETIQUETTE

A few helpful pointers for etiquette are offered here concerning the standard dinner set up at your table. Traditional etiquette dictates that you do not begin to eat a course until everyone at the table has been served. Many of the cruise ships and the finer restaurants follow the same formal dinner setting that you experience aboard ship. The waiter normally places your napkin on your lap as soon as you sit down at the table. Your napkin should remain folded in half on your lap throughout the meal between periodic uses. When you leave the table, your napkin should be placed loosely at the left of your place setting.

Each placement of flatware has a specific purpose. There can be as many as twelve or more pieces of flatware at your plate. Here is a quick rule of thumb for using flatware. For the setting of utensils on either side of your plate, you should work from the outside in. For the setting of utensils above your dinner plate, work from the top of the plate in an upward fashion. Your bread plate is always on your left and your drinking glasses are always slightly above your plate and to your right. For wines, hold a white wine by the stem of the glass so that you do not affect the chill of the wine. Hold a red wine by the base of the bulb. Coffee is not normally ordered until after dinner, but may be requested earlier if desired.

For a full course dinner the following is suggested, and is considered socially accepted for use of your utensils. They are listed in the order you normally use them:

Appetizer: Use the salad/pivot fork from your outside left and auxiliary knife from your outside right. If you have ordered salad, save the salad/pivot fork and auxiliary knife by placing them on your bread and butter plate. (Note: in some instances the waiter may replace the salad fork and auxiliary knife.)

Soup: Use the soup spoon taken from your right. When you are finished with the soup, place your soup spoon on the side of the soup plate farthest away from you.

Salad: Use the salad/pivot fork and auxiliary knife that you saved by placing them on your bread plate after your appetizer course.

Main Course: Use the large knife and fork closest to your dinner plate in the lower setting. When you temporarily stop eating, you can place your knife and fork in the five and seven o'clock positions on your plate. When you are finished with the course, place your knife and fork in a parallel five o'clock position, with the cutting blade of the knife pointed toward you. The waiter should know to pick-up your plate. In some cases, a fish knife will be supplied on your right.

Cheeses: Use the dessert fork and dessert knife in the upper setting of utensils, above and closest to your dinner plate.

Dessert: Use the small fork or compote spoon in the upper setting of utensils, above the dinner plate. Baked Alaska may be eaten with a fork or spoon.

Coffee/Tea: Use the teaspoon/demitasse spoon in the upper setting above and farthest away from your dinner plate.

The above is provided only for your information. Most of all, enjoy your dinner! No one is going to notice, or care, what utensil you use.

Most ships prepare a designated special midnight buffet as an extravaganza featuring a gourmet's delight. The chef's galley takes considerable pride in preparing the appetizing food along with special ice carvings and sculptures. It is a breath-taking sight! Just prior to the time to partake in the buffet, thirty or so minutes are devoted to allowing everyone to walk through and take photos of the way food is prepared and wonderfully presented. Be sure to walk through the display and take your pictures, but please move through quickly because the viewing is short and the chef tries to start the buffet on time.

GRATUITIES (Only a Guideline)

Tipping sometimes is a sensitive subject with people. Even in a fine restaurant people may disagree over what to leave. Tips are not normally included in the cruise fare except on certain luxury ships. Check with your travel agent. On your cruise, tipping is made very easy. Tipping is expected, but should be given at the sole discretion of each individual guest commensurate with the level of services performed. A suggested minimum guideline is offered here. Tips, as appropriate, are normally given at the end of the cruise on the last night.

Cabin Steward:	*$3.00 -or more per day per person (as desired).
Waiter:	*$3.00 -or more per day per person (as desired).
Assistant Waiter:	*$1.75 -or more per day per person (as desired).
Butler:	*$2.00 -or more per day per person (as desired for suites)

*Some passengers tip more and some less.

Tipping remaining service personnel such as the maitre d', room service and head waiter are at your discretion, but a daily gratuity is not necessary. For salon or spa personnel, a 15% gratuity is normal. For bar drinks, sodas, and wines, a 15% gratuity is usually added to each bill. In some instances this gratuity may not be added, check first.

You can contact the Purser for envelopes, or on the next to last evening of the cruise, the cabin steward may place several envelopes in your room along with the next day's bulletin. You can label these envelopes and then place in each envelope the amount you desire to give each person who served you. Change can be requested at the Purser's desk.

When you leave your cabin for dinner on the last evening of the cruise, hand the cabin steward an envelope or leave it on your bed where it is easily visible. Carry the other envelopes to dinner with you. After dinner, specifically hand the envelope to the appropriate person. Of course, this is all done at your discretion. The preceding is provided only for your information.

You do not see the cabin steward often, but excellent results of his/her work is always evident and the steward is certainly deserving of recognition. You leave your cabin in the morning for a brisk walk or breakfast and when you return, the beds are made, there are fresh towels and your cabin is spotless. During the day the cabin steward sees to all your cabin needs, including laundry or dry cleaning for a charge. When you have dressed for the evening and leave for dinner and the night festivities, the cabin steward slips into your cabin. Towels are replaced and the cabin is in order again. Your beds are turned down, chocolates placed on your pillows and a daily bulletin left for the next day's activities. Your cabin is warm and welcoming to return to. Wow, what a life!

On some cruise ships such as the Holland America Line, they say that tipping is not required and that the crew is there to serve. What this really means is tipping is not solicited, but is accepted and normally should be awarded. If service has been good, tips should be given; and aboard ship service is seldom, if ever, poor. Many times if service appears not to be excellent, it is usually caused by a language barrier or a mis-communication.

CHAPTER TEN

SHIPBOARD ACTIVITIES

ENTERTAINMENT

Expect everything on board a ship to be similar to a five star resort hotel. The ship will have fine cuisine, a casino, swimming pools, hot tubs, spa services, sauna, fitness center, walking or jogging track, golf (or golf simulator), informative lectures and theater. They will have dancing, live music, midnight buffet, night clubs, D.J. disco, bars and lounges, wine tasting, duty-free shops, theme nights, parties for singles and honeymooners, Broadway shows, superb service, outstanding entertainment, a library and even places for quiet time.

Ships have excellent activities for teens and kids. There is something for everyone! If a teenager travels with you, encourage him/her to attend the first meeting for teens. The ship will announce a teenage get-together which will provide an overview of activities and things to come. It also encourages teens to meet others they may choose to "hangout" with. If, after the first meeting, they choose not to participate, then so be it.

Be sure to have pre teenage children become involved with the ship activities. Most cruise ships have special programs for younger children, usually from age three to 17 or 18. Check with your travel agent at the time you are considering the booking to determine which ships best accommodate younger children. Be sure to manage your children while on board ship. Their safety could be jeopardized if they are allowed to run free on the ship. Not only that, but also, young children who are rowdy and running loose through the ship disturb other paying passengers. Safety and consideration for others is always important. There are sitters on board who can be contracted for an evening.

Always refer to the daily guide for the next day's activities. It will tell you what is available during the next day both on board and at the next port to be visited. Review this guide either that evening or the first thing the next morning. While the ladies are getting ready, guys can review the daily guide. Take the guide to breakfast with you and read over it very carefully. Unfortunately, some passengers overlook reading the daily bulletin. They never know what is available to them and what the dress is for dinner. Good advice is to fold one and always carry it with you. Extra bulletins can be picked up at the Purser's desk.

KEEPING IN SHAPE

Cruise ships provide gourmet food that is hard to refuse. However, they also offer a way to keep the weight down during the cruise with light food and especially their fitness program. Each ship has its own program and ways to reward your participation with fitness. Some issue you a card or booklet that can be punched, stamped or initialed. Others will hand you a fitness coupon every time you participate in a fitness session.

At the end of the cruise you can turn these coupons or cards in for prizes. There are scheduled exercise and aerobics classes that are excellent for staying in shape. The fitness center will have stationary bicycles, weights, tread mills, step machines and other exercise equipment. There are normally two decks to walk or jog on. Get up in the morning and do some walking or jogging, also in the early evening before dinner. Use the stairs instead of the elevators as much as possible. This is a good way to keep the weight down because you are likely to gain a pound or two. A few passengers have been known to lose a couple of pounds on a cruise. Stay healthy on your cruise and enjoy it. Also, ships have substance abuse meetings.

GAMES AND CASINO

Ships will have a daily quiz that can be picked up during the morning in the library. These are brain teasers that challenge you to answer questions on sports, history, geography, music, trivia, science, literary arts, entertainment and other areas of interest. When you are in your stateroom the television presents interesting information along with movies that can be enjoyed. When in port, the casino and shops will be closed. Once the ship sails away from ports, the casino and shopping arcade will be open for business. Slots and gambling tables are available if you desire. According to the many people interviewed, the pay-out is not quite as good as Las Vegas, but it is still fun to try. Passengers must be 18 to gamble. Drinks are served only to passengers 21 and over. Disney ships do not have a casino.

Various activities are available for everyone. It just depends on what you want to do with the time you have on board ship. And the time goes very fast, so enjoy. A three or four day cruise ends before you really get accustomed to the new life. A seven day cruise is just right for some, but others will want to continue the "high life" because they are not ready to leave the ship.

During the course of the cruise, the ship's hotel and dining facilities offer excellent atmosphere, service and normally there is no charge for juices, milk, tea or regular coffee. There are so many areas for entertainment, fun, excitement, music, shows, education. It would be difficult to name them all here. To mention a few other activities, there are lectures on various ports of call, and on different subjects, there are junior and teen parties, tours of the ship, tournaments, all kinds of games for prizes, hair, beauty and fitness demonstrations, mileage pool guesses, ice carving demonstration, learn to play Blackjack, Craps, the slots and Roulette, art auctions, sing along, Karaoke, afternoon teas, Ping-pong, bingo, shuffle board, golf putting competition, bridge, gin rummy, fashion show, dance classes, horse races and the list goes on. The Cruise Director has the goal and experience to provide high quality entertainment to all cruise passengers with different tastes.

Most ships offer religious services. This can be a nondenominational service. However in some cases Protestant, Catholic and/or Jewish services may be offered on cruises longer than seven days. Information concerning the services is provided in the daily activity sheet.

SAFETY AND RULES

This is an important section. However, many passengers to the cruise world feel that if they pay their fare they should be entitled to do pretty much what they want to do. Airlines have rules and regulations that must be directed by the aircraft Captain and further carried out and enforced by the flight attendants. Sometimes passengers resent some of the rules that are in place for their safety and the good of airline travel, but the Federal Aviation Agency sees fit to enforce certain rules for the comfort and safety of all passengers on the aircraft.

Although not directly applicable to the exact same way airline travel is conducted, cruise travel has certain rules and requirements that passengers must follow and at other times there are codes and guide lines that passengers should follow. For those very few who may seriously violate another passenger or crew member, ships do have security officials and even a small confinement facility.

LIFEBOAT DRILL

The cruise line is required by international law to have certain emergency equipment on board. The Coast Guard and the Safety of Life at Sea (SOLAS) requires a drill practice within 24 hours of embarkation. Normally, this will be held prior to sailing. All passengers are to either take or don life vests and report to the mustering station on the Captain's signal, and then may be directed to the designated area near the assigned life boat. The life vests are located either on your stateroom bed or in the cabin closet. If you have children with you, have a child's life jacket in the room or make arrangements for one. The instructions are on the back of your cabin entrance door and are usually shown on the television in your stateroom immediately after you board.

SHIPBOARD ACTIVITIES

A crew member will explain how the drill will be executed. Then through the ship's speakers, the Captain will speak from the bridge and explain the signal to don life jackets and report to the mustering stations. At this signal, passengers must follow the instructions and proceed to their assigned mustering station, usually out on deck. This is a fun thing to do and a roll call by stateroom may be made at the life boats to insure all passengers participate. Cooperate fully with the ship's crew for this drill. You will actually enjoy it! Follow the directions given by the crew members. Those who do not attend for one reason or another will be contacted after the drill.

In the event of an actual emergency, you will be directed on what to take with you. This normally consists of a floatation vest, blanket, hat and your medical supplies, if required. Articles taken depends somewhat on your geographical area also. For the drill, take only your floatation vest or as the crew directs. The ship's crew members are well trained to handle any emergency in the unlikely event that one could happen. They help usher you along your way to the proper station. Have fun with this drill, but keep in mind the seriousness of it. Know where to report and how to get there safely and quickly. Sometime during the cruise, when most of the passengers are on shore at a port, the crew will conduct an exercise on their own with simulated emergencies. The Captain will announce such an exercise and then ring the alarm bell (usually seven short rings and one long ring).

Inform the Purser if you or a member of your party have any physical problems that would slow them down for the evacuation. A crew member will normally be sent to assist.

GENERAL SHIP OPERATING PROCEDURES

There are certain areas on a ship where passengers are not allowed. The engine room is off-limits to passengers for security and insurance reasons. For safety reasons various other areas aboard ship are off limits such as the Bridge where the Captain and his staff command and operate the ship. In some cases, the Captain will offer an invitation for a certain time period for passengers to tour the bridge. This is normally announced either in the daily bulletin or by special invitation. You may be asked to sign up for the tour ahead of time so that control can be made for the visit. The bridge is fascinating and it is highly recommended you visit this area if you have never seen one. The state of the art for the equipment a ship's Captain has at his finger tips for ship management, control, navigation and safety is extremely interesting.

For the safety of the ship and for environmental concerns, cruise lines request that you do not throw lighted cigarettes, cigars, pipe ashes or any other item off the side of the ship. The burning ash could be sucked into an opening in the ship's side or open deck and burn someone or cause a fire. Throwing trash into the ocean is not an environmental proper thing to do either. Cruise lines take steps to protect the environment and especially at-risk ports of call.

Ship lines recognize that there are both smokers and nonsmokers. To handle the difference, ships have designated smoking and non-smoking areas and passengers are requested to thoughtfully observe them. Pipe and cigar smoking is normally not permitted except on an outer deck such as the Promenade Deck, verandas or in a designated area. Cruise lines have policies on smoking, but sometimes are hesitant to enforce them.

SHIP'S CREW

There are normally three major categories for operations aboard ship: (1) Officers, (2) Staff and (3) Crew. Command and operation of the ship is directed by the officers. Activities aboard ship are laid out by the cruise staff. The personnel who make-up these positions generally approximates slightly less than one half of the number of passengers. To give you an idea of the ship's senior officers the following is offered.

Cruise lines uniform insignias vary, but normally senior officers wearing four stripes on their sleeve and epaulette/shoulder board consist of the Captain, Staff Captain, Chief Engineer, Hotel Manager, and Chief Purser. The Captain wears one of his four stripes wider than the remaining three.

Captain: The Captain is the absolute master who has all power, control and management rights. The Captain has had years of training, experience and is "signed" for the ship, crew and passenger safety.

Staff Captain: The Staff Captain is second in command. This position works closely with the Captain and can take over in the Captain's absence. He is also addressed as "Captain." On small ships if there is not a Staff Captain, this position is filled by a First Mate.

Chief Engineer: Has responsibilities for all the mechanical well-being of the ship. He holds the maritime rank of "Captain."

Hotel Manager: Supervises the majority of the ship's crew. He has the extensive responsibility for all service provided on the ship; similar to a large land hotel manager. The Hotel Manager shares some responsibilities with the Chief Purser.

Chief Purser: The Chief Purser is not only the "bean counter" (financial officer), but takes care of the administration, business, accommodations and information center. The Chief Purser also handles customs and immigration formalities.

Maritime officers wear stripes on their epaulets or at the base of their jacket sleeves. A brief description of the traditional stripes and colors, if added, is as follows:

Deck Officers:	Diamond	No color
Hotel Officers:	Clover leaf	White
Engineering:	Propeller	Purple
Medical:	Hermes Staff	Red
Communications:	Radio signal	Green
Security:	"S"	Brown to Red

These officers have the major operations/command responsibilities to the cruise line headquarters for the safety and effectiveness of the ship. Of course, the Captain is ultimately responsible. The "buck stops" with him as he has absolute control. Officers pretty much have the run of the ship with their management responsibilities. The staff and crew handle most of the remaining details to operate the ship, provide entertainment, service and accommodate passenger needs.

Keep in mind, for the cause of safety, the Captain has authority to cancel any port stops whenever he deems it necessary because of weather, labor disputes on shore, mechanical problems or for any other safety reasons. Sometimes this upsets passengers, but safety is paramount.

Many times the Cruise Director acts socially on behalf of the Captain. When in uniform he/she has three stripes reporting to a four stripe officer, usually the Hotel Manager. The Cruise Director is assisted by the Assistant Cruise Director and Cruise Staff for entertainment functions. Among other duties, the Social Hostess who does not hold an officer rank, assists the Captain and senior officers at social functions. Social and management obligations often take the Captain away from the bridge, therefore the Staff Captain will be in charge at any given time. You will find the ship's officers to be extremely interested in your safety, well-being and in solving your problems; work with them. You will see them continuously about the ship looking after the ship operations and crew effectiveness.

ON BOARD SHOPPING

Shopping aboard ship is a fun experience. The shops, along with the casino, are open when the ship is away from ports and at sea. When you are not in the casino or playing bingo, sitting by the pool or attending other functions, it is fun to browse through the ship's gifts, souvenir, jewelry, fashion and fragrance shops. This is nice for the gentlemen because they can be doing "guy things" while the mother, wife, daughter or girlfriend is shopping. The ship guarantees its products and a few ships will match a price that an item is offered at any of its ports when proof is shown. During a visit at a port, if you purchase an item at a shop recommended by the cruise line, within a certain number of days, normally 30, that purchase is guaranteed against defects or damage in shipment. Purchases that are returned due to "buyers' regret" are NOT normally covered.

CHAPTER ELEVEN

EXCURSIONS AND PORT ACTIVITIES

THE CRUISE PACKAGE

When you receive your cruise package from your travel agent fifteen to twenty days or so before the cruise date, it will contain your tickets, registration forms and a booklet that lists the tours offered during the course of your cruise. This is a good time to review the tours that will be available to later help you with your selection. A good description of each tour will be given along with the time duration, type of activity required such as riding, walking, climbing, level of difficulty, if any, and the price. Some may require considerable physical effort. It is important to go over the descriptions of the tours very carefully so you will understand them. Consider your physical ability before selecting a specific tour. Normally you will not select the tours until after you board the ship, except on certain cruises.

On overseas cruises such as to Europe and to other countries the tour information may be sent early with the opportunity to pre-book. This will be done through your travel agent.

It is not necessary to take a tour at each port. It is nice to relax, enjoy yourself and companions and select only the tours that especially interest you. Sometimes it is more relaxing to take your time and casually look over a port without a tour. If you are able to get around fairly well, you can tour the area on your own. Usually there will be a taxi or minibus available that can be hired for a personal tour if you desire, but be cautious as to the agreed price and make sure there is a reputable driver. Insure you agree on the price of the tour, where it takes you and what time you will return before you accept it. If the vehicle breaks down on your tour you have booked separately from the ship and you cannot make the ship's departure time, you may be left on shore. In this case, make every attempt to contact the port authority. Unfortunately, it is still up to the Captain whether to wait on you. Generally, if you are going on a tour, it is safer to book through the ship even though the tour may be slightly more expensive than one booked on shore. If you have visited a place before and there is only a certain area you want to visit, then consider a private tour on your own or share the price with another couple or two.

There are times when you may sail with people who have been to the particular area before and are familiar with the tours. Word of mouth is a good way to determine if a tour is

EXCURSIONS AND PORT ACTIVITIES

worth the price and if the viewing is what you want to see. Occasionally, you may go on a tour that is not quite what it is advertised to be and the tour may disappoint you, although this is the exception rather than the rule. For the most part, the tours are excellent. If you have a problem on any tour, be sure and report it to the ship's tour desk. If away from the ship and you are a swimmer, stick with swimming in the salt water and sea or chlorinated swimming pools. Unless a particular lake or river has been declared clean and safe, do not swim there.

As pointed out in an earlier chapter, a cruise is what you make it. If you continually hurry about to do everything, it may not be relaxing. At times, it is nice to remain on the ship when you visit a port. You can read, swim, sit by the pool, attend a movie or other function, take a nap and, of course, you can always eat delicious food! A nap may sound foolish or a loss of time, but after three or four days on the ship, getting up fairly early and staying up late, a nap comes in handy. Another possibility is to go off the ship and just walk around the local area. Or if necessary take a cab to the downtown shopping area. This way you can return to the ship when you desire.

BOOKING THE TOURS

Let's assume this is your first trip into a certain port and you are not sure what to do. People aboard ship will be helpful. Some may have been on tours at the port in question and will offer some advice.

Attendants at the ship's excursion desk are acquainted with the tours. Most ships have a briefing on the tours by showing videos, giving detailed descriptions and information. Information on places to visit or shop are also available on your cabin television. By attending the tours overview, held in the showroom, the Port Lecturer will give you a better idea of what to do and where to shop. This briefing will be announced in your daily bulletin.

For your first visit, you will not go wrong with a city or town tour. Certain tours will be more popular than others. Perhaps the next time you visit the port you could take a tour that goes further away or to an area that is not associated directly with the port where the ship is docked. There are numerous options available.

Do not be afraid of missing the ship because of tours you have booked through the ship. The tours are all timed so as to return and drop you off in town or back at the ship prior to sailing time. If the ship-booked tour bus has a flat tire or some emergency, the ship will wait on you. If you book a tour on your own, make sure the tour guide knows what time you must be back so you will be returned on time. Do not be late or you may be left high and dry as the ship will not wait. Normally, you will not have a problem. Do not delay in making your reservations for the tours. Some may fill up and you will have to select a second or third choice.

TENDERING

If a ship is unable to dock at a port, the ship's crew will tender the passengers to shore. This is done by the cruise staff or Excursion Desk handing out tender tickets. These are free and are numbered according to the time you will board a tender for transportation to shore. The numbers on the tickets will be called out in order and passengers will report to the tender area for boarding when their number is called. On large ships, several tenders may be used and the operation goes very smoothly. Boarding the tenders is a simple process in calm seas. There are always crew members present to assist. Sometimes tendering will dock you near the center of a town, such as St. Thomas, and a taxi will not be necessary.

Physically challenged passengers must travel with someone who is able to assist them both at sea and on shore. The cruise lines are unable to supply a crew member for this assistance. Guests confined to wheelchairs may not be able to go ashore by tender in some cases such as during rough seas. It may be too dangerous. The ship's Captain has the last word on this decision. Under smooth sea conditions, passengers in wheelchairs are permitted to go ashore by tender.

Some ships such as Royal Caribbean's "Grandeur of the Seas" can employ an automated system which allows the ship to stay in place without lowering the anchor while tendering. This is due to a system called dynamic positioning. It uses the Global Positioning System (GPS) method. The ship's thrusters keep it in position while tendering. The method can be used in calm seas when there isn't a lot of wind. This is good also for the ecology of the ocean floor; especially around sensitive islands such as the Cayman Islands. Although Captains are cautious, large ship anchors can damage the coral reefs and various underwater sea deposits.

PORT SHOPPING

The Port Lecturer will advise you of reputable shops, good buys at a port, places for lunch and what to watch out for. What you need to know, and even carry with you, are the prices of goods of interest back home for a comparison. You may not save on some stones, jewelry, crystal, cameras, fragrances, china, art or electronics during your cruise. Before you leave home check prices. Sometimes you can do as well, price wise, at home. Many of the items at shops in the Caribbean are negotiable. Check prices at two or more stores.

TIME CHANGES

Occasionally, when you sail in an east or west direction, you will travel through time change zones. Insure that you know whether there is a different time ashore as compared to the ship's time so you will not be a victim of being late because of the difference in time. This has happened to passengers before. If there is a time difference it will always be included in the daily activity schedule and the Cruise Director will announce and emphasize the time difference during one or more of the entertainment sessions. Read and keep the daily activity schedule with you.

CHAPTER TWELVE

DISEMBARKATION

THE CRUISE CONCLUSION

Disembarkation, if not properly managed, can be somewhat frustrating. At the conclusion of the cruise when the cruise ship arrives at the port with a large number of passengers, the disembarkation must be properly managed and supervised. Passengers cannot disembark all at once. Being aware of the procedures will allow this operation to run smoothly for you. It is simply not true that the larger the ship the more difficult it is to embark and disembark. The secret is how these two operations are managed.

An orderly passenger exit of the ship must be imposed by the ship's crew. Some ships may have a large number of passengers to transfer from the ship to the terminal. If this exit or disembarkation procedure is not carefully executed there can be crowding and confusion. A few days into the cruise you will be asked to fill out a form to include the airline or travel reservations you have at the conclusion of the cruise. Depending on the time and the day you are leaving the city will affect the time that you will be released from the ship to go ashore.

In a meeting or on your television the next to last day of the cruise, you will be briefed by the Cruise Director on how customs, immigration, agriculture, luggage handling, cruise questionnaire, tipping, finance requirements, disembarkation and all other associated areas will be handled. The briefing is normally held in the large showroom and is delivered, somewhat, with a sense of humor. At least one member of your party should attend this meeting as it defines all the elements to complete the cruise and the disembarkation. The briefing may be repeated on your cabin television.

Usually, if a meeting is held in the theater, staff and crew members who were key service people will be called upon the stage and be presented for your appreciation for their work during the cruise. These could be the entertainers, cruise staff, stewards, head waiters and perhaps the chefs may be presented for their outstanding culinary work. These crew members work very hard to pamper you and do deserve credit.

The cabin steward will provide you with a Cruise Questionnaire which he places in your cabin. Take the time to fill out the questionnaire. This has a special significance to the cruise line and to you. It puts you on their mailing list for special rates for cruises in the future. It also gives you a

DISEMBARKATION

chance to rate the food, service, entertainment and certain crew members you feel deserve special credit. The cruise line takes the information on this questionnaire very seriously. Also, on the morning of disembarkation, they may have drawings from the questionnaires for prizes.

PREPARING TO DISEMBARK

The day before disembarkation, the cabin steward will have given you certain color tags to be placed on your luggage. You will use this color/number to determine when you are to report to the deck and gangway area for exiting the ship. The day of disembarkation, listen for your color/number to be called over the loud speaker for reporting to the appropriate deck to exit the ship.

The last night, just prior to the morning arrival of the ship at the final destination, there are significant actions for preparation of your disembarkation. This preparation is all explained by the Cruise Director. A further explanation is offered here. You will be requested to pack all your clothes and belongings EXCEPT what you are going to wear off the ship the next day. Also retain the toilet articles and sleepwear you will require. Place remaining clothing in your luggage, attach the proper tags and set the luggage in the hall next to your cabin door for pick up during the night. This MUST be done before you go to bed the last night of the cruise. It is a good idea to have a lock on each piece of luggage. Do not place cartons of tax-exempt booze outside your door with the luggage as the cabin at the end of the hall will have a big "leaving the ship party" the last night.

In Chapter Seven, Packing tips and suggested packing checklist, on the "Seven Day Cruise Ladies and Gentlemen, General Items", there is listed an item, "One medium or small carry-on bag for the last night's cruise." This bag is used for your sleep wear and toilet articles to be used the last night and morning before disembarkation. This you will hand-carry. Again, be sure to keep one set of clothes to wear off the ship. Do not place all your clothes in the luggage that is picked up the night before or it will be extremely embarrassing the next day when you have nothing to wear! This has happened in the past and a passenger had to wrap a blanket around himself with only his pajamas to be escorted to the baggage area to retrieve his clothes. Pajamas, undershorts or a night gown are just not proper attire to wear ashore!

The breakfast hours will be somewhat earlier than usual the morning you arrive at the end of the cruise. This is done so the ship's crew can begin to prepare the ship for the new set of passengers. You will also be asked to vacate your cabin at a certain time, normally by 9:00 AM, to allow the cabin steward to prepare the cabin for the next cruise. The crew will be very busy during this time and may not be quite as attentive as during the cruise.

DISEMBARKATION

Immigration officials will board the ship and all non citizens must personally report to the designated on board immigration area before the ship can be released for passenger debarkation.

If the ship docks in the morning between 7:00 AM and 9:00 AM and you have an airline departure near 12:00 noon, you will most likely be in the second or third group of people authorized to leave the ship. This is only fair. If you have an airline reservation later that afternoon or the next day, you will most likely be in a group to leave a few minutes later. Most cruise lines are very efficient at disembarking passengers and as a rule nearly all will be off the ship in a couple of hours after disembarkation begins. It slows the process to crowd around the deck and the exit area where the disembarkation is taking place. This action only delays the orderly procedures put into effect by the ship's crew. It is best to go to a common area where you can sit, relax, even wait topside and talk with fellow passengers until they call your color/number.

The disembarkation can be a simple procedure if everyone follows the directions given by the ship's personnel. The procedure may start with airline connection times, but there are also other factors affecting disembarkation. Certain VIP or suite occupied personnel and normally physically challenged passengers could have early priority to disembark. There is a cruise line protocol for the disembarkation procedures.

The baggage areas within the terminal will be identified by signs with numbers and/or colors. Luggage picked up the night before aboard ship with the color and/or number codes attached will be placed at these stations so that luggage can be easily located. Porters will normally be available in the terminal to help you with your luggage. If you use a porter, they expect a tip. It may be announced that if you have the air/sea package, your luggage can be sent directly to the airport. Check this out so you will know.

When you disembark from the ship be sure to have your customs declaration form with you. You *must fill this form out before you leave the ship* so it can be turned into the customs officials as you exit the ship. Custom procedures were explained thoroughly at the Cruise Director's briefing the day before. Custom officials will spot check luggage at any time. Stick to your custom allowance and *do not transport fruit or vegetables off the ship in any of your bags. You can be fined for this.*

Transportation procedures will be announced prior to debarkation. There will be personnel outside the terminal to assist you in finding your transportation. The cruise line will furnish transportation to the airport or hotel if you have the air/sea package. Otherwise you would have to pay approximately $10.00 to $20.00 per person to use their mode of transportation. If you have previously chosen to rent a car, the rental agency will transfer you to the rental car office to pick up your automobile. If neither of these apply then it is up to you to take a taxi, bus or be picked up in some other way.

This all sounds rather involved and complicated, but it is not. The procedures are explained in detail. There is always someone who is anxious to help you. When you are not sure as to what to do, just ask a cruise line representative.

WRAP-UP

Wrap-up your cruise by saying good-by to special people you have met during the cruise. This should also include any crew member/staff who was special to you. Be sure and check your cabin thoroughly for all your belongings. If the cabin contained a safe, make sure you leave it open when you leave. Leave your door keys/cards in the room unless they are personalized. Insure that you have all your travel documents in your hands or in your carry-on bag.

...And no, you can not take the waiter, assistant waiter or cabin steward home with you!

When you arrive at home you will normally be quite tired. Allow yourself at least one day of late get-up and rest before returning to work. The early and late hours aboard ship and the transportation home will catch up with you when you finally reach your home. Disembarkation, transportation and getting home are the toughest parts of a cruise.

Beginning with your first cruise, start a photo album of strictly cruise and tour photos. You will enjoy them for years to come.

...AGAIN, HAPPY CRUISING!

APPENDIX

NAUTICAL GLOSSARY

Abeam	At or from the side of the ship. At right angle to its length.
Aboveboard	Areas of the ship above the waterline.
Aft	Near, toward or in the rear of the ship
Air-Cruise	Total cost package of air, cruise and ground travel to and from the port including transfers.
Ahead	In front of the ship's bow.
Aloft	Above the ship's superstructure.
Amidships	In or towards the middle of the ship, lengthwise.
Alleyway	a corridor or passageway.
Anchor ball	Black ball hoisted above the bow to show that the ship is anchored.
Astern	Beyond the ship's stern.
Backwash	Movement of the water when the propellers are in reverse.
Ballast	Extra weight placed below for better stability.
Batten Down	To secure all open hatches or equipment while under way.
Beam	Width of the ship between its two sides at its widest point.
Below	Any area beneath the main deck.

Bearing	Compass direction in degrees from the ship to a point.
Berth	Dock, pier, quay (key); also a bed inside a cabin.
Bilge	Lowest space within the structure of a ship or boat.
Binnacle	Ship's compass.
Boat	Generally a craft less than 65 feet, sail or power. Some boats can be carried on a ship, such as a lifeboat. However, submarines are called "boats". Princess "Love Boats" are actually ships. (Commercial name.)
Boat Stations	The space near the lifeboat where a person reports during a lifeboat drill or emergency.
Boatswain	A warrant or petty officer in charge of a ship's deck crew, rigging, cables and anchors. Also, may be called a bos'n or bosun.
Bow	Front or forward portion of a ship.
Bowthruster	Screw to propel ship sideways.
Bridge	Command and navigation control center of a ship.
Bulkhead	Upright partition dividing the ship into compartments.
Bulwark	Ship's outer wall.
Bunkers	Fuel storage area. Bunkering means taking on fuel.
Cabin	Stateroom, living area.

Capstan	Spindle for storing ropes and cables.
Cast off	Release lines prior to sailing.
Category	The price level of a cabin based on location.
CDC	Center for Disease Control and Prevention.
Cleat	Device to attach lines, ropes etc.
Coaming	Raised lip or curb at ship's doors and hatches to keep water out.
Colors	Ship's emblem or national flag.
Companionway	Interior stairway.
Course	Ship's direction in compass degrees.
Christen a Ship:	The custom of breaking a bottle of wine or champagne at the stem of a new ship along with a good toast or blessing is done so that bottle can never again be used with a toast to wish ill will on the ship. Therefore, the blessing or toast is good for ever.
Cruise Only	The fare you pay is strictly for the cruise only. Any and all ground or air transportation is paid by you.
CS	"Club Ship" concept.
Davit	A device for raising and lowering lifeboats.
Disembark	Depart the ship, as to shore.

Displacement Tonnage	The volume of water displaced by a ship. The weight of the water displaced being equal to the weight of the vessel displacing it.
Dock	Berth, pier or quay (key). The act of bringing the ship to dock.
Draft	Distance from a ship's waterline to the bottom of its keel.
DS	Diesel Ship.
Embark	To enter or go aboard the ship.
Even Keel	The ship in a true vertical position as opposed to listing to one side.
Fantail	The rear overhang of the ship.
Fathom	Distance of depth, one fathom equals six feet.
Flagstaff	A pole with a flag of the ship's country of registry. This is placed at the stern of the ship.
Air/sea	Total cost package of flying, cruising and ground travel to and from the port including transfers.
Fore	The forward mast or front (bow) of the ship.
Forward	Towards the front (bow) of the ship.
Free port	Port/place exempt from customs duty.
Funnel	The smokestack or chimney of the ship.

Galleon	A large three-masted sailing ship having two or more decks used in the 15th and 16th century, especially by Spain. Used for war or commerce.
Galley	Ship's kitchen.
Gangway	Ramp by which passengers enter and leave a ship.
Gross Registered Tons/Tonnes (GRT)	A passenger ship's tonnage is calculated by space and not weight. It is the total of enclosed spaces, excluding the bridge, radio room, galleys plus other designated areas for commanding the ship. One GRT equals 100 cubic feet of enclosed space, and is the basis how port and other costs are determined. Also see Passenger Space Ratio (PSR).
"Growlers"	Small icebergs.
Hatch	Cover leading to a hold.
Hawser	Large rope for securing a ship at dock, or towing a ship
Helm	The entire steering equipment center.
Hold	Interior space below the main deck normally towards the bottom of the ship.
House Flag	The flag denoting the ship's company.
Hull	The shell or framework of the ship excluding superstructure or masts..
IB	Ice breaker.

I.M.O.	Abbreviation for International Maritime Organization, governing body for safety and other standards at sea.
Inaugural	The early or first part of a new ship's cruising after being launched.
Inboard	Towards the center of the ship. Sometimes associated with inside cabins without an ocean view.
Jones Act	An old Passenger Service Act originally designed to protect American passenger hauling. It does not permit any foreign flag ship to transport people between two points in the U.S. without at least stopping at one foreign port in between. A cruise line can be fined for not abiding by it. It is considered antiquated by many.
Keel	The longitudinal center of the ship's underside. Aides balance.
Knot	A unit of speed only. As "20 knots or nautical miles per hour." A nautical mile is approximately 1.15 statute miles. A nautical mile is equal to one-sixtieth of a degree of the earth's circumference and is 6,080.2 feet as opposed to a statute mile which is 5,280 feet.
Landlubber	Person who is unfamiliar with sailing and the sea.
Latitude	Denotes the distance in degrees, minutes and seconds north or south of the equator

League	Measure of distance. A league is approximately 3 statute miles or 3.45 nautical miles.
Leeward	Side of a ship or other element that is sheltered from the wind.
Line	Usually a rope smaller than a larger rope (hawser) or cable used in mooring or towing a ship.
List	To lean to one side.
Longitude	Denotes distance in degrees, minutes and seconds east or west of "0" degree at the Greenwich Observatory, London. At the Equator, one minute of longitude is equal to one nautical mile. As the longitude meridians converge nearing the poles, the size of a degree becomes smaller. A mid range may be used to more accurately measure a specific earth's distance.
Maiden Voyage	Ship's first official cruise.
Maitre d'Hotel	The manager or head steward of a restaurant/hotel (dinning room).
Manifest	A list of a ship's passengers, cargo and crew.
MARPOL	Standards, which are promulgated by the International Convention for the Prevention of Pollution from Ships. The MARPOL Treaty is an international law governing waste disposal in a marine environment.
MS	Motor ship (uses diesel oil).
MSY	Motor sailing yacht.

MTS	Motor turbine ship (steam), or motor twin screw (diesel).
Muster	To assemble passengers and crew.
MV	Motor vessel (diesel) has piston engine.
Muster Station	Muster assembly point as in an emergency. Usually assigned.
MY	Motor yacht.
MYS	Motor yacht sailing.
Nautical Mile	Approximately 6,080.2 feet and 1.15 of a statute mile. Conforms more to the earth's surface which is one sixtieth of a degree of the circumference of the earth.
Open Seating	For passengers to have the access to any table at any time during appointed hours.
Outboard	Towards, at or beyond the ship's sides.
Paddlewheel	Commonly used on riverboats. A wheel of boards which paddle the boat forward or aft.
Passenger Space Ratio (PSR)	A measurement of cubic space per passenger. GRT divided by the number of passengers (basis of two per cabin) equals PSR. A PSR of 50:1 or above is the ultimate in roominess; 49 to 40 is spacious; 39 to 30 is very good; and below 30 is high density (not free flowing space). (Also see GRT)

Pax	Abbreviation for passengers.
Pilot	A person licensed to advise the captain of another ship on handling his ship in and out of ports or harbors.
Pitch	A rocking motion up and down, bow to stern when waves cause such motion.
Port	Left side of the ship when on the ship facing forward. Derived from early days sailing when ships would come against a port/dock on the left side.
Port Charges	Charges usually collected by the cruise line which must be paid to authorities in ports to cover surcharges and fees. Port charges are normally included in the cruise fare.
Port Tax	A charge required by a port local government.
Porthole	A circular window on a ship.
P.O.S.H	Acronym for "Port Out, Starboard Home". It was derived from the more expensive cabins on the England to India cruise route. These cabins were believed to be more shaded from the hot sun.
Propellers	Screws. Sometime expressed as variable pitch or fixed pitch.
Prow	The bow or the stem of the ship.
Purser	A position on board ship that is responsible for financial and administrative duties.
Quarterdeck	The rear section of the upper deck.

Quay	Pier, dock or berth (pronounced "key").
Refit	A refreshing, remodeling, face lift or redecoration of a ship. The refit can be done in wetdock or drydock.
Registry	The country the ship is registered in. Its owners must comply with their law as well as the laws of other countries visited.
Repositioning Cruise	An interim itinerary that takes a ship from one season's cruising to another. Usually the price of a cruise is slightly less for a reposition cruise.
Rigging	The ropes, lines, cables and chains that support the ship's masts, spars, posts, cranes etc.
RMS	Royal Mail Ship (sometimes referred to as Royal Majesty Ship).
Roll	The alternate sway of a ship from side to side. The ship's horizontal stabilizers dampen this movement.
Rudder	The steering device at the stern and below the water line.
Running Lights	Consists of three lights that must be lit if the ship is sailing at night. Lights are green on the starboard, red on the portside and white at the top of the ship's mast.
Screw	Ship's propeller.
Second Seating	The later of two meal times in the ship's dining room.

Shell Door	The outer door just above water line that allows pilots, gangways and access to stores.
Ship	Varies in length from approximately 100 feet up and carries approximately 100 or more passengers.
Sounding	Measurement of water depth.
Space Ratio	The passenger space ratio computes to the density of a ship. It is derived by dividing the number of passengers (basis of two) into the gross registered tonnage of a ship. An answer of 50 or above is excellent (low density); 49 to 40 is very good; 39 to 30 is good, but average and below 30 denotes a higher density.
SS	Steam Ship
SSC	Semi-submersible craft
Stabilizer	A gyroscopically operated wing-like device extending from both sides of the ship below the waterline. Its purpose is to provide stability for the ship in reducing roll by tilting as much as 20 degrees each in opposite directions. Roll sometimes tends to encourage motion/seasickness. The stabilizers are retracted when entering a port.
Stack	The funnel or chimney where the ship's gases are freed.
Starboard	When aboard the ship, facing the bow, starboard is the right side of the ship. Derived from early days sailing when certain ships had a "steering

	board" suspended over the right side of the ship which acted as a rudder. This was abbreviated to starboard. So as not to damage the "steering board", ships would dock on the left side or port side.
Stateroom	Another term for a ship's cabin.
Statute Mile	Used on land and is 5,280 feet.
Stem	The extreme bow or prow of the ship.
Stern	The extreme rear/back/aft of the ship.
Steward	Personnel on board a ship. Usually refers to the cabin attendant.
Stow	To load with personal belongings, cargo or provisions.
STR	Abbreviation for Steamer.
STS	Sail training ship.
Superstructure	The structure of the ship above the main deck or water line.
SV	Sailing vessel.
SY	Sailing yacht.
TBA.	Abbreviation of to be assigned or announced.
Tender	Small boat, which could be a lifeboat or used to transfer passengers and crew to and from shore when the ship is at anchor.
TES	Turbo-electric ship (steam).

Thrusters	Propellers normally positioned forward below the water line on a ship and used to move a ship sideways away from a dock.
Transfers	Transportation between the ship and airports, hotels and excursions.
TS	Twin screw. Also, Turbine ship/steamer (similar to TSS).
TSMV	Twin-screw motor vessel. May be diesel-electric.
TSS	Turbine steamship (uses heavy fuel oil).
TTS	Twin turbine screw.
U.S.P.H.	Abbreviation of United States Public Health for inspections and prevention of disease.
Under Way	When the ship has departed or is in the process of departing.
Upper Berth	A single size bed usually folded into the wall or ceiling during the day. Normally above the floor.
Wake	A trail of disturbed water left behind a moving ship.
Watch	A period (usually four hours) in which is spent on duty for the safe operation of the ship.
Waterline	The line along side the ship's hull that meets the surface of the water.
Weigh	To raise or move, as to weigh anchor.
Wheelhouse	The bridge and center for command and navigation.

Windward	Side of the ship or element towards the wind.
Yacht	A luxury type vessel with sleek and/or graceful lines. Generally have lengths greater than 40 feet with sail or power.
Yaw	To move unsteadily and turn about the vertical axis of the ship. May cause temporary deviation in rough seas. Can be measured in degrees.
YS	Yacht ship.

INDEX

Air/Sea Packages, 140
Alaska, 54, 56
American Hawaii, 111
Antarctica, 55
Arctic, 56
Balcony/Veranda, 19, 40
Baltic, 55
Barge "Cruising," 136
Bermuda, 54, 63
Black Sea, 55
Boarding Procedures 163
Booking Tours, 204
Booking, 20, 39
Brochures, 13
Cabin Selection, 16
Cabin Steward, 186
Canada/New England, 55, 64
Cancellations, 45
Caribbean, 54, 58
Carnival Cruise Lines, 105
Carry-on Bags, 149, 150, 157
Car Use, 29
Celebrity Cruises, 92
Commodore Cruise Line, 69
Common Sense, 33
Communications, 27
Contracting a Cruise, 13, 42
Costa Cruises, 102
Cruise Conclusion, 208
Cruise Deposit, 43
Cruise Experience, 20
Cruise Mate Card, 24
Cruise Mates & Notes, 234
Cruise Package, 201
Cruise Ship Pricing, 69
Cruise Ship Size, 71
Cruise World, 1
Crystal Cruises, 119

Cunard Line, Ltd., 121
Customs, 213
Delta Queen Cruises, 132
Dining, 178
Dining Room Etiquette, 181
Dinner Dress Guide, 156
Disembarkation, 208
Disney Cruise Line, 98
Dress for Gentlemen, 155
Dress for Ladies, 152
Dress & Etiquette, 174
Eastern Caribbean, 59
Economy Season, 52
Embarkation, 162
Entertainment, 188
Excursions Activities, 201
Freighter & Cargo Ships, 137
Games and Casino, 191
Grading Ships, 80
Gratuities Guide, 184
Great Britain, 55
Greenland, 56
Hawaii, 55
Holiday Cruise, 52
Holland America Line, 84
Holy Land, 56
Honeymooners, 22
Hotel Safety Tips, 146
Iceland, 56
Inaugural Season, 50
Insurance, 47
Internet, 16
Keeping in Shape, 190
Knots and Log, 172
Large Ships, 71
Late Contract, 49
Learning the Ship, 167
Lifeboat Drill, 193

INDEX

Luxury Cruise Lines, 114
Luxury Ships, 113
Locator Card, 169
Maiden Voyage, 50
Medical Preparations, 26
Mediterranean, 55
Medium Ships, 71
Mega-Ships, 71
Mexico, 54
Mid-Price Ships, 73
Motion/Sea Sickness, 25
Nautical Glossary, 217
Navigation, 10
New England/Canada, 64
Northern Europe, 55
Norwegian Cruise Line, 100
On board Shopping, 199
Orient Lines, 109
Orient, 56
Overseas River Cruises, 136
Overseas, 67
Packing Checklist, 157
Packing Tips, 148
Panama Canal, 54, 65
Passenger Age Scale, 81
Passenger Space Ratio, 82
Peak Season, 52
Planning Your Arrival, 162
Planning Your Cruise, 12
Port Shopping, 206
Preparing for a Cruise, 23
Preparing to Disembark, 210
Princess Cruises, 95
Radisson Seven Seas, 124
Reorders, 235
Reposition Cruise, 52
River Cruise Cities, 134

River Cruises, 132
Royal Caribbean, 88
Safety and Environment, 8
Safety and Rules, 192
Scandinavia, 56
Seabourn Cruise Line, 126
Select a Line & Ship, 69
Selecting an Itinerary, 14, 52
Sense of Direction, 31
Sense of Humor, 31
Sense of Purpose, 31
Packing List for Men, 158
Packing list for Ladies, 159
Ship Ops Procedures, 195
Ship Per Diem, 34
Ship Photos, 115-118
Ship Selection, 77
Ship's Crew, 196
Shipboard Activities, 188
Ship's Dress & Dining, 174
Shopping, 199, 206
Silversea Cruises, 128
Small Ships, 71
South America, 56
South Pacific, 56
Southeast Asia, 56
Southern Caribbean, 61
Steamboat Regions, 133
Suggested Packing List, 157
Tall Ships, 130
Tendering, 205
Theme Cruises, 51, 100
Things to do at Home, 160
Thumbnail of Mid Ships, 73
Time Changes, 207
Time to Book, 20
Transportation & Hotels, 140

INDEX

Travel Agent, 34
Travel Documents, 28
Travel Packet, 28, 45
Travel Sense, 30
Types of Cruises, 50
Using Dinner Flatware, 181
Valuables, 166
Value Season, 52
Veendam Location Card, 169
Western Caribbean, 60
What's Right for You, 75
Where Ships are Built, 72
Where/When to Cruise, 53
Windstar Cruises, 130
Wrap-up, 214

"CRUISE MATES" AND NOTES

Names, addresses, phone numbers, name of the ship and dates of sailing with my "Cruise Mates:"

REORDERS:

TO ORDER COPIES OF THE BOOK

CRUISE MATE...
AND THE VOYAGE CONTINUES

MAIL:

Please send a check, <u>print</u> your name and address and send to:

PONY PUBLISHING
10532 STONEFLOWER DRIVE, STE 33
PARKER, CO 80134

PHONE:

Telephone: 1-800-859-3910

Enclose a check for $12.75 for each copy. Add $2.00 postage for the first book and $.50 postage for each additional book.

A discount is allowed for an order of five books, the sixth book is free. For more than six books, phone for a quote.

If you have any corrections, comments or additions to this book, please contact Pony Publishing by mail. Comments will be considered for subsequent editions.